The Role of Twitter in the 2016 US Election

"Is the Twitter-fueled rise of Donald Trump in 2016 a harbinger of the future or a one-time event? *The Role of Twitter in the 2016 Presidential Election* brings together valuable assessments of the role of Twitter in 2016 and beyond in a timely effort to understand how Twitter mattered then and how it may matter in the future. Social media is not going away, and political scientists and campaigns both need to better understand its implications. This book is a useful first step in that direction."
—**David P. Redlawsk**, *James R. Soles Professor, Political Science, University of Delaware, USA*

"The expansive use of Twitter by candidates, political organizations, the media, and the public was the most significant development in the evolution of the new media campaign in 2016. This timely and important volume provides a context for understanding how Twitter became a force in American politics, and sorts out the complicated, often mystifying, use of Twitter by Donald Trump. The authors address these issues from a range of disciplinary approaches, and provide unique and diverse insights. A must-read for political communication scholars and students as well as campaign practitioners."
—**Diana Owen**, *Associate Professor, Political Science, Georgetown University, USA*

"Twitter contains a lot of noise, but also a good deal of signal about modern American politics. These chapters skillfully examine how politicians communicate their campaign messages and policy stances in 140 characters while appealing to specific groups of voters and earning free media. The authors focus on our first Twitter president, but also note how other candidates adapt their own approaches. This is vital reading for understanding modern campaign communications and 2016 in particular."
—**Seth Masket**, *Professor, Political Science, University of Denver, USA*

"One cannot understand the Trump phenomenon without understanding Twitter's role in his rise. This book provides essential material for the layman seeking just that understanding. Trump's Tweets were different from those of prior candidates and from Tweets of his competition, a portion of the media and the public responded, and in a close election, it may have made the difference. Campaign communication may never be the same again, and this book helps us understand why."
—**Jeremy D. Mayer**, *Associate Professor, Schar School of Policy and Government, George Mason University, USA*

Christopher J. Galdieri • Jennifer C. Lucas •
Tauna S. Sisco
Editors

The Role of Twitter in the 2016 US Election

Editors
Christopher J. Galdieri
Saint Anselm College
Manchester, New Hampshire
USA

Jennifer C. Lucas
Saint Anselm College
Manchester, New Hampshire
USA

Tauna S. Sisco
Saint Anselm College
Manchester, New Hampshire
USA

ISBN 978-3-319-68980-7   ISBN 978-3-319-68981-4   (eBook)
https://doi.org/10.1007/978-3-319-68981-4

Library of Congress Control Number: 2017955264

Cover illustration: Abstract Bricks and Shadows
© Stephen Bonk/Fotolia.co.uk

Printed on acid-free paper

This Palgrave Pivot imprint is published by Springer Nature
The registered company is Springer International Publishing AG
The registered company address is: Gewerbestrasse 11, 6330 Cham, Switzerland

ACKNOWLEDGMENTS

In March 2017, scholars from across the country gathered at the third *American Elections Conference* at the New Hampshire Institute of Politics on the campus of Saint Anselm College. This book was inspired by a session on social media and the national election. We are grateful to the conference participants for their novel discussion on a new form of campaign communication. This conference would not have been possible without generous contributions of the Politics and Sociology Departments at Saint Anselm College, prior conference organizers Dr. Peter Josephson and Dr. Ward Holder, and our colleagues who graciously moderated panels. Further, we would like to personally thank Katelyn Ellison, Lorie Cochran, and Brandon Pratt for their hard work and dedication.

This work would not have been possible without the support of the Vice President for Academic Affairs Office at Saint Anselm College and the New Hampshire Institute of Politics. We are especially indebted to Br. Isaac Murphy, OSB, Vice President of Academic Affairs; Dr. Mark Cronin, Dean of the College; and Mr. Neil Levesque, Executive Director of the New Hampshire Institute of Politics.

We would like to thank our editor at Palgrave Pivot, Michelle Chen, Editorial Assistant John Stegner, and the entire editorial and production staff.

Finally, thank you to our partners, Kate, Dave, and Jim, with special thanks to our tiniest supporters: Veronica, Adelaide, Desmond, James, Sebastian, and Gabriel.

Contents

About the Authors

Notes on Editors

Christopher J. Galdieri is Associate Professor of Politics at Saint Anselm College. He received his undergraduate degree from Georgetown University and his doctorate from the University of Minnesota. He is a frequent commentator on New Hampshire and presidential primary politics and has published in *Politics and Policy*, *New England Journal of Political Science*, *Columbia Journalism Review*, and several edited volumes.

Jennifer C. Lucas is Professor of Politics at Saint Anselm College. She holds a PhD from the University of Maryland—College Park. Her research, which focuses on the role of gender in campaigns, public policy, and congressional politics, has appeared in *Politics & Gender*, *American Politics Research*, and *Social Science Quarterly*. She is also the former co-editor of the *Journal of Women, Politics, and Policy*.

Tauna S. Sisco is Chair and Associate Professor of Sociology at Saint Anselm College. She received her doctorate from Purdue University. Her research on women, politics, and public policy has appeared in *Feminist Media Studies*, *The Journal of Women, Politics, and Policy*, and several chapters in edited volumes. Her work also includes the *Homeless Access Survey*, a five-year research study and publications with the New Hampshire Department of Health and Human Services, Bureau of Housing and Homelessness, which assessed the needs and access of the New Hampshire adult homeless populations.

Notes on Contributors

Todd L. Belt is Professor of Political Science at the University of Hawaii at Hilo. His research and writing focuses on the mass media, public opinion, the presidency, campaigns, and elections. His is the co-author of four books and has published over a dozen chapters in edited scholarly books and over two dozen scholarly articles. He holds a PhD from the University of Southern California and is the recipient of two teaching awards.

Tyler Cote is a senior in the Honors College, University of Massachusetts Lowell. His research on political rhetoric has been published in *The Forum: A Journal of Applied Research in Contemporary Politics.*

Tyler Farley is a senior in the Honors College, University of Massachusetts Lowell. His research has been published in the *Journal of Law & Courts* and *The Forum: A Journal of Applied Research in Contemporary Politics.*

J. Scott Granberg-Rademacker is Professor of Political Science and Public Administration at Minnesota State University, Mankato. His current research focuses on the impact of Twitter on campaigns and elections.

Kim Hixson is Department Head of Journalism and Communication at Utah State University. He previously served as Chair of the Communication Department at the University of Wisconsin-Whitewater. He holds a PhD from the Southern Illinois University. His research interests are social media in politics and media uses and gratifications. Hixson's experience also includes serving two terms in the Wisconsin legislature (pre-Scott Walker).

Paul Joyce is a 2017 graduate of the government program at Utica College and currently a Masters of Public Administration candidate at Rockefeller College, The University of Albany.

Morgan Marietta is Associate Professor of Political Science at the University of Massachusetts Lowell and author of *The Politics of Sacred Rhetoric: Absolutist Appeals and Political Persuasion, A Citizen's Guide to American Ideology: Conservatism and Liberalism in Contemporary Politics, A Citizen's Guide to the Constitution and the Supreme Court: Constitutional Conflict in*

American Politics, and the forthcoming *One Nation, Two Realities: Dueling Facts in American Democracy*.

Paul Murphy is a senior in the Honors College, University of Massachusetts Lowell. His research on political rhetoric has been published in *The Forum: A Journal of Applied Research in Contemporary Politics*.

Mark J. O'Gorman is Professor of Political Science and Environmental Studies Program Coordinator at Maryville College (MC) in East Tennessee. O'Gorman was part of the team whose efforts earned MC a *Sierra* Magazine "Cool Schools" distinction for the college's excellence in environmental sustainability. His academic publications include work on renewable energy, environmentally focused economic development, and environmental security. O'Gorman has advised the Obama administration's Council on Environmental Quality (CEQ) and has been a frequent on-air US elections expert for Tennessee media. His book chapter on the Obama Administration's environmental record was published in the predecessor to this text, *The American Election 2012*. O'Gorman holds a PhD from the Maxwell School of Citizenship and Public Affairs at Syracuse University.

Kevin Parsneau is Associate Professor in the Department of Government at Minnesota State University, Mankato, where he teaches US politics, the presidency, and public administration. He researches the presidency, executive branch nominations, campaigns and primaries, and party elites, and his research has appeared in *American Politics Research*, *Politics and Policy*, and the *New England Journal of Political Science*. He received his doctorate from the University of Minnesota and his undergraduate degree from the University of Montana.

Luke Perry is Chair and Associate Professor of Government at Utica College and Director of the Utica College Center of Public Affairs and Election Research. His scholarly focus is presidential elections and religion and politics. His most recent book will be out next year examining religious responses to marriage equality across the political and religious spectrum. In addition to his academic work, Perry is an election analyst for WKTV News Channel 2 and national political columnist for the *Utica Observer Dispatch*. He was a correspondent on the floor of both national party conventions and the presidential inauguration.

ABBREVIATIONS AND ACRONYMS

ANES   American National Election Survey
AGW   Anthropogenic global warming
BLS   Bureau of Labor Statistics
CC   Climate change
EPA   Environmental Protection Agency
gcc   global climate change
GHG   greenhouse gas
g.w.   global warming
SNL   Saturday Night Live

LIST OF FIGURES

LIST OF TABLES

CHAPTER 1

Introduction: Politics in 140 Characters or Less

Christopher J. Galdieri, Jennifer C. Lucas, and Tauna S. Sisco

Abstract These chapters are based on research presented at the third *American Elections* conference held at the New Hampshire Institute of Politics on the campus of Saint Anselm College. They come from scholars of political science, communications, public policy, and political psychology. They deploy a diverse set of methods to examine various facets of Twitter's role in the last election and shed light on the ways in which Twitter will continue to affect the course of modern American politics, 140 characters at a time.

Keywords Twitter • 140 characters • American politics

Every few decades, presidents and candidates for president upend American politics by turning new technology into a potent political weapon. Consider how Franklin Roosevelt used the radio to hold "fireside chats" with a Depression-wracked American public, or how John F. Kennedy and Ronald Reagan used their superior understanding of the visual component of television to build support for themselves and to stymie their political opponents. More recently, twenty-first century presidential candidates like John McCain in 2000, Howard Dean in 2004, and Barack Obama in 2008

C.J. Galdieri (✉) • J.C. Lucas • T.S. Sisco
Saint Anselm College, Manchester, NH, USA

© The Author(s) 2018
C.J. Galdieri et al. (eds.), *The Role of Twitter in the 2016 US Election*,
https://doi.org/10.1007/978-3-319-68981-4_1

1

each broke new ground in the use of small-donor fundraising and voter contact through the internet. These candidates continued a long tradition of communications technology impacting American politics that stretches all the way back to the pamphleteers whose stoking of the fires of the American revolution was possible thanks to the invention of the printing press.

To this list we must now add Donald Trump, whose use of Twitter—the social networking platform through which users can broadcast their thoughts to the world in 140-character morsels known as "tweets"—was crucial to his political rise and his unlikely victory in the 2016 presidential election. Trump is not the first politician to use Twitter since it was launched in 2006; having a Twitter presence has become as necessary for a presidential candidate as having a web site, television ads, and campaign volunteers. But Trump's use of the platform was—and continues to be—unique. Before becoming a candidate, Trump used Twitter to turn himself from a real estate mogul turned reality show host into a political gadfly, propagating absurd, racist conspiracy theories about President Obama's birthplace and citizenship and weighing in on other political developments. As a candidate in 2016, some of Trump's late-night (or early-morning) tweets set the terms of a day's morning news cycle. Other tweets took aim at his opponents in the Republican primary and in the general election, or at reporters, news organizations, and even private citizens who criticized him or his campaign.

Twitter has been such an important part of Trump's political persona for so long that we risk forgetting how unusual it is, just as many Americans may rarely stop and consider how bizarre it is that Donald Trump, object of endless New York tabloid newspaper coverage and *Spy* magazine parodies when he entered the national conversation in the 1980s, now occupies the White House. This volume represents a first attempt to consider the impact Twitter had on the 2016 presidential election, both at the hands of Donald Trump and at those of the other candidates who sought the presidency in that contest. The impact has already been felt beyond the election, as Trump's social media habits have continued in the transition from campaigning to governing. Only six months into his presidency, a Fox News poll found that only 13% of voters approved of his tweets (Blanton 2017).

In the second chapter in this volume, Marietta, Cote, Farley, and Murphy explore the background of Twitter and argue that aspects of Twitter favor each of the two major parties in different ways. They argue that for each side to tweet effectively, they need to focus on simplicity and threats. Indeed, they demonstrate, by analyzing retweeted messages, Clinton's focus on examples of oppression, a type of issue where her party's message is straightforward, while Trump emphasized threats. On the flip side of that argument, and more surprisingly, Trump did not emphasize the economy, since the conservative economic argument relies on a more complex set of arguments. Clinton did not emphasize foreign policy and terrorism for a similar reason, while Trump was more likely to do so.

In Chap. 3, Granberg-Rademacker and Parsneau delve into the early part of the 2016 campaign by examining tweets from before the Iowa caucus through Super Tuesday. Their analysis suggests that where the candidates stood in the race determined their Twitter strategy, with Clinton's front-runner status meaning fewer tweets, aimed more at the other party, with an eye toward the general election. Sanders, as the challenger to the front-runner, tweeted significantly more. Republicans, on the other hand, had to deal with a large primary field, so were more often focused on intra-party conflict. This resulted in significant partisan differences, with Trump and Cruz attacking their primary opponents more, and Democratic candidates Sanders and Clinton focused more on policy. The authors demonstrate that while Trump focused on Twitter to attack primary opponents and his own party, other candidates used Twitter to make policy statements, promote their organizational efforts, or provide informational tweets. However, among voters it was Sanders and Trump who generated the most enthusi-asm as measured through retweets.

In Chap. 4, Kim Hixon argues that Trump's tweets can provide insight into his character and image. Unsurprisingly, the main candidate image attributes identified in Trump's primary tweets are anger/aggressiveness and confidence. He also analyzes which image attributes gained earned media or free publicity. Comparing this subset of earned media tweets to all the tweets reveals a difference between the candidate-projected image and the media-projected image of Trump. One-third of Trump's tweets contained the anger/aggressive attribute, but a much higher percentage of these tweets was mentioned in the newspaper articles. The media coverage of Trump's tweets helped him have a much higher value in earned media than his opponents. This advantage, coupled with his victories, leads to questions about how Trump's tweets will affect candidate messaging and candidate image in future campaigns.

Chapter 5 gives us an overview of the what, when, and how of Trump's Twitter habits. For the "when," Perry and Joyce demonstrate that a quarter of Trump's tweeting occurred in the morning, influencing the nature of the traditional news cycle by coming just in time for the morning cable news shows. The "how" includes a good deal of exclamation points and all capital letters, while the "what" includes primarily negativity and criticisms of his ubiquitous opponents. However, it was those negative or all caps tweets that were often among the most popular. Trump's ability to attract news coverage may have been linked to both the timing of his tweets and their popularity, particularly the most controversial ones.

Mark O'Gorman in Chap. 6 examines Trump's environmental policy tweets, particularly the frequency, form, and function of tweets related to global warming and climate change. This is especially interesting given Trump's evolution on this issue from his concern during the time before he became a presidential candidate to claiming it is a hoax as his presidential run neared. Surprisingly, he only tweeted once about global warming while officially a presidential candidate. However, during the Obama Administration, Trump's 144 global warming or climate change tweets were all negative and used his unusual style of tweeting. Finally, O'Gorman analyzes the misconceptions about climate change in Trump's tweets and catalogs his revisionist environmental policy.

Chapter 7 concludes the book by comparing humorous political images on Twitter and other social media outlets. These images can frame issues and make a clear statement about candidates in a way that is easy for anyone to comprehend, regardless of their level of political interest. These images can also promote or hinder the level of polarized conflict or use of gender stereotypes, as well as evoke emotions. Was Twitter used similarly to other forms of social media, or did it stand out? Todd Belt determines that while most images were used to attack political candidates and figures regardless of source, political images on Twitter were slightly more partisan, less likely to employ masculine stereotypes, and less emotionally evocative than other social media outlets. This speaks to Twitter's particular format and audience. Humorous political images on Twitter are likely to appeal to a more politically informed and educated audience, compared to sites like Facebook.

Twitter's impact is such an overwhelming fact of modern American politics that it has obscured attention to *how* it impacts politics. This volume is a first effort at studying the role Twitter played in the 2016, and how this social media platform enabled Trump's rise and affected citizen politics. Above and beyond Trump's use of Twitter, there is also the question of how his rivals and other Twitter users engaged in political activity through the platform. To what extent did candidates use Twitter to communicate with their supporters? How did their supporters respond? And what of citizens' own political engagement on Twitter?

These chapters are based on research presented at the third *American Elections* conference held at the New Hampshire Institute of Politics on the campus of Saint Anselm College. They come from scholars of political science, communications, public policy, and political psychology. They deploy a diverse set of methods to examine various facets of Twitter's role in the last election and shed light on the ways in which Twitter will continue to affect the course of modern American politics, 140 characters at a time.

REFERENCE

Blanton, Dana. 2017. Fox News Poll: Voters Say Tweets Hurting Trump's Agenda. *Fox News*, June 29. Online at http://www.foxnews.com/politics/2017/06/29/fox-news-poll-voters-say-trumps-tweets-hurting-agenda.html. Accessed 8 Aug 2017.

CHAPTER 2

Less Is More Ideological: Conservative and Liberal Communication on Twitter in the 2016 Race

Morgan Marietta, Tyler Cote, Tyler Farley, and Paul Murphy

Abstract Prior to the 2016 race, Twitter was seen as a more Democratic than Republican campaign platform. In light of the extraordinary use of social media by the Trump campaign, this chapter examines how ideological communication by either faction can be advanced or limited within this medium. We argue that the simplest and most inciting aspects of each ideology can be communicated clearly, but not the more complex or mundane facets. This suggests that certain issues will be emphasized and others neglected on Twitter by each side. These hypotheses are borne out in the 2016 Twitter campaigns, in which Clinton and Trump focused on only specific aspects and issues of the competing ideologies, and followers retweeted in a similar pattern. In the Twitter campaign, less can indeed be more ideological when the ideologies are communicated in their reduced forms.

Keywords Ideology • Social media • Twitter • Psychology of threats • Engagement

M. Marietta (✉) • T. Cote • T. Farley • P. Murphy
University of Massachusetts, Lowell, MA, USA

© The Author(s) 2018
C.J. Galdieri et al. (eds.), *The Role of Twitter in the 2016 US Election*,
https://doi.org/10.1007/978-3-319-68981-4_2

7

Now, tweeting happens to be a modern day form of communication. You can like it or not. Between Facebook and Twitter, I have 25 million people. It's a very effective way of communication.
(Donald Trump, 2nd Presidential Debate, 9 October 2016)

Two decades ago, John Petrocik introduced the concept of issue ownership in American politics: parties hold specific divisive issues as their campaign property (Petrocik 1996). Whenever the issue arises, the landlord party is advantaged (Republicans own national security, while Democrats own health care). Since then it has become clear that certain media can be owned by one side of the ideological aisle as well. Conservatives have maintained effective ownership of talk radio for several decades (Barker 2002). The most prominent newspapers are more controlled by the left (*New York Times, The Washington Post*). Cable news has effectively split into competing camps (Fox News vs. MSNBC). The newer medium of Twitter seems to be up for grabs. This chapter addresses what the 2016 election suggests about the ideological and partisan path Twitter will follow.

There were several reasons prior to the 2016 campaign to suspect that the rise of Twitter as a normal means of campaign communication would advantage liberals over conservatives. The rise of Facebook has certainly been seen as an advantage for Democratic communication, fund-raising, and mobilization. Twitter users are decidedly younger than the rest of the voting population, giving Democrats an opening advantage. And conservatives have raised complaints (especially online) that right-wing voices have been silenced on Twitter and other social media, leading some conservative pundits to advocate leaving social media to the left and focusing on recognized conservative platforms.[1] With these observations in mind, the prominent use of Twitter by the Trump campaign is a surprising development, leading to the question of the ideological future of the medium. When we examine the Twitter format and contemporary political ideology, we argue that aspects of Twitter advantage certain facets of each ideology. Twitter as a campaign medium can be employed effectively for ideological communication by either side, but only when invoking the *simple* and *inciting* aspects of their ideological message. When we compare Clinton's and Trump's use of Twitter during the 2016 campaign, these patterns are confirmed. The participation by ordinary citizens over Twitter (gauged by their rate of retweeting a candidate's messages) follows a similar pattern, suggesting that the specific ideological messages facilitated by Twitter are effective in communicating to voters. To understand these patterns, we may need to begin with the nature of Twitter and the nature of contemporary ideology.

THE NATURE OF TWITTER

It has been said that brevity is not the soul of wit; crudity is. Twitter offers both. Our question is what this means about this new form of campaign communication. Twitter has at least two outstanding characteristics as a form of campaign communication: it is *brief* and situated within an *entertainment* medium. Each of these characteristics shapes its political potential. The brevity of a tweet may seem to limit expression, but as Gross and Johnson describe it, the 140-character format can be a "liberating constraint" (2016: 748). Enforced brevity may also be liberating clarity, free from the expectation or possibility of detail or nuance. Twitter leaves little space for dodging or fence-sitting, known vices of politicians.[2] The brief format channels expression into the simplest part of each competing ideology; what is simple can be expressed, while what is complex cannot.

The second characteristic of Twitter is its broader context. Political tweets are situated *within* an entertainment medium, even if they are not always entertaining. And that competition is the shaping influence. On Twitter, Democrats are competing not only against Republicans but also against music, sports, movies, television, comedians, friends, and every other thing that pops up on a citizen's Twitter feed. If a tweet is not amusing or otherwise attention-grabbing, it is often quickly left behind. Aside from humor, another path to attention is incitement. Insults or controversial statements will gain attention. For this reason, political tweets are likely to include negative attacks on the opposing candidate.[3] They are also more likely to invoke the most emotion-laden, morally meaningful, or provoking aspects of a candidate's platform. While most political tweets will be seen only by citizens following a candidate's Twitter feed, those that succeed at being amusing, challenging, or inciting are more likely to be discussed by mainstream media.[4] Each tweet is free, but only some generate additional free media.[5] Twitter advantages and encourages the *simple* and *inciting* aspects of each political ideology.

THE NATURE OF CONTEMPORARY IDEOLOGY

Which aspects of contemporary conservatism and liberalism are the simplest and most inciting? To answer that question, we have to look at the core aspects of each competing ideology. In current polarized America, ideologues seem more likely to talk past than to understand each other, especially when we recognize that the two competing ideologies do not ask the same question and offer different answers, but instead pose different core questions.[6] Conservatism sees our society as fundamentally fragile, facing a host of internal and external enemies that challenge our desire for ordered liberty (the combination of liberty with responsibility), which demands the appropriate balance between freedom and authority. The answers to the core question of conservatism—how do we glue together a free and fragile society?—lead to the competing branches of conservatism. Economic conservatives believe that property and work ethic are the answers to the glue problem; national defense conservatives believe it is patriotism and a strong military; social conservatives believe it is religion and a shared moral system, while cultural conservatives believe it is tradition, which includes a shared language. Liberalism, on the other hand, perceives society as fundamentally perfectible, with a better world reflecting greater equality and social justice. The core goal is to lessen oppression, or the systematic denial of achievement and status; the oppressed groups we must help are somewhat in dispute, but the leading contenders are the poor, Blacks, Hispanics, women, and LGBT. Traditional liberals believe that the core source of oppression is poverty (e.g., Bernie Sanders), while multiculturalists believe the core source of oppression is identity. Hillary Clinton seems more likely to be in the multicultural faction, something that her pattern of tweeting may illuminate.

The ideology of Trumpism as opposed to the persona of Trump has taken some time for commentators to recognize, given his lack of prior elective office. Trump is surely not a conservative along the lines of George W. Bush or of Ronald Reagan, or of the editors of *National Review* and the *Weekly Standard*, many of whom were never-Trumpers. But nonetheless, Trump can be described as a conservative, though one not like his opponents for the Republican nomination. Trump is primarily a cultural conservative, whose answer to the glue problem is tradition and shared language. Trump's overt nationalism is an aspect of this branch of conservatism, which colors most of his policy perspectives. His signature issue is immigration, which is the core concern of cultural conservatism. Trump sees economic policy through the lens of nationalism: protection of American jobs, anti-free trade, beating other countries in deals. His foreign policy is also nationalist: America-first, no ideological wars, make allies pay for protection. And of course Trump's views on immigration are nationalist: limit immigration from the southern border and refugees from the Middle East. In Trump's view, past policies on immigration have increased competition for low-wage jobs, are altering English as the national language, are raising public costs for social services, and are lowering our security from crime and terrorism. Trump is an economic, immigration, and foreign policy nationalist, or a cultural conservative who sees multiple threats to national power, traditions, and stability.

THE INTERSECTION OF TWITTER AND IDEOLOGY

Some scholars have argued that liberalism is more complex than conservatism. If this were true, conservatism would be advantaged on Twitter, as the simpler set of ideas to express. The complex causal nature of liberalism would be harder to fit into brief and inciting tweets. However, the view that conservatism is the simple ideology is too simple.[7] Conservatism argues for straightforward, non-complex causation in some realms, while liberalism argues for a complex and nuanced causation of events; but in other realms it is the reverse. Consider the difference between terrorism and the minimum wage. The conservative response to terrorism is simple and straightforward: there are people who hate us; kill them before they come here; employ surveillance of individuals and mosques that may pose a threat, which is more important than concerns about civil liberties. The liberal response is more complex: we must consider the origins of the violence, especially the US role in it; we must engage in improving the image of the United States abroad in order to prevent future attacks; we must especially avoid blaming one religion for terrorism, which increases oppression of Muslims within the United States and outside, increasing the dangers of future terror attacks. Responding to terrorism is more complex than military retaliation. This pattern does not hold, however, when we turn to the minimum wage. The liberal view is the more simple and straightforward one: hardworking people deserve a living wage; raise the minimum wage so they can have a decent standard of living; corporations can afford to pay it, and arguments to the contrary are driven by greed and lack of compassion. Conservatives take the more complex and difficult to explain causal position: raising the minimum wage may sound compassionate, but there will be unintended negative consequences; higher wages will cause higher unemployment among low-skill workers; some businesses will go under or have greater incentives to seek mechanization of low-skill jobs; and the result will be declining aggregate income for people at the lower end of the economic ladder, exactly the people the new laws are meant to help. Each ideology has more simple and more complex aspects. Our hypothesis is that Twitter can communicate most effectively the simple aspect of either ideology, which suggests an emphasis on different policy domains by each side in their campaign tweets.

The second aspect of Twitter that frames ideological communication is the incentive to be inciting. Each ideology has arguments and concerns that are more emotional, morally disturbing, and create a more visceral response. These are the aspects of the belief system that Twitter privileges. Likely the simplest and most inciting message of cultural conservatism is *threat*. This is perhaps the most provocative aspect of the ideology, invoking the fear of internal and external enemies. There are threats to security, to jobs, to the national economy, to cultural longevity, to peace on the streets. Threat has been recognized as a powerful motivator of political decision-making and engagement. Threat penetrates political inattention; it invokes emotion, encouraging non-rational processing; and it bolsters in-group identification, all of which combine to increase political participation and preferences for strong leadership (see especially Albertson and Gadarian 2015; Boyer and Parren 2015; Gadarian 2010; Landau et al. 2004; Merolla and Zechmeister 2013; Pyszczynski et al. 2003). The political psychology literature identifies several different forms of perceived threats that can create these effects, including threats to

(A) *Personal Security:* potential physical violence; "concerns surrounding physical or material safety" (Schmid and Muldoon 2015)

(B) *Individual Status:* potential lowering of personal well-being, either absolute or relative, including "economic threat" (Onraet et al. 2013), "fear of unemployment" (Feldman and Stenner 1997), or threats to the "professional identity" of blue-collar workers "by taking jobs involving routinized work tasks that are not consistent with the creativity and improvisation involved in craftsmanship" (Petriglieri 2011)

(C) *Group Status:* potential lowering of the well-being or respect accorded to one's identity group, including "threats surrounding positive distinctiveness or status" (Schmid and Muldoon 2015), "potential harm to the values, meanings, or enactments of an identity" (Petriglieri 2011), or "the subjective perception that out-group members pose a threat to valued resources or preferred states of affairs" (Bobo 1983)

While these types of threats are diverse, they *all* were invoked in Trump's rhetoric. Economic insecurity, terrorism, and immigration were three of the main themes of the Trump campaign, creating opportunity to invoke threats to *personal security* from terrorist violence and crimes committed by undocumented immigrants, threats to *individual status* from economic decline and from job loss to recent arrivals, and threats to *group status* from comparative loss to immigrant groups. Past campaigns have invoked clear or subtle threats in some categories, but Trump hit *all* of them repeatedly and without subtlety. In this sense, he is one of the most—and possibly *the* most—threat-inducing presidential candidate of post-WWII American politics, which fits with his ideological perspective.[8] With this in mind, we could expect Trump's use of Twitter to focus on the invocation of threat rather than the more complex aspects of conservatism.

On the liberal side, it is a different set of concerns that are simple and inciting. The clearest concern of liberalism is *social justice*, pointing out the oppression of specific groups. This argument can be communicated very quickly and accurately, especially through the use of specific examples of oppression grounded in poverty, race, ethnicity, gender, or sexual orientation. The liberal (and Democratic Party) approach to solving oppression is also straightforward: expel racism and racists and provide government protection for minorities and financial support for the poor. These policies are implicit in the liberal worldview once oppression is demonstrated (while conservatives tend to argue that poverty is not easily removed and the attempt to alter social conditions will often have unintended consequences). While examples of oppression and the violation of social justice can be pointed out in very brief language—"Another unarmed Black man was shot in a police incident. This should be intolerable. We have so much work to do #TerenceCrutcher –H" (20 September 2016)—they also invoke emotion and outrage. Twitter as a campaign format may be especially suited to examples of social injustice and the communication of threats, the simple and inciting aspects of each ideology.

TRUMP VERSUS CLINTON IN 2016

If these hypotheses are correct, we should see clear differences in emphasis between the Clinton and Trump tweets. Clinton would focus on examples of oppression, while Trump would emphasize threats. Both would employ negative attacks on their opponent. Perhaps more surprisingly, Trump would *not* emphasize the economy, as the more complex set of conservative arguments, even though jobs and trade were a signature part of his campaign strategy. Clinton would *not* emphasize foreign policy and terrorism, while Trump would be more likely to do so.

To gauge the role of these domains in the 2016 Twitter campaign, we examined the 100 most retweeted messages from Clinton and from Trump during the presidential campaign season from 1 June 2016 to 7 November 2016.[9] The results are displayed in Table 2.1. Listening to media reports during the campaign season, a casual follower of politics may have gained the impression that Donald Trump was out-tweeting Hillary Clinton. His use of Twitter certainly gained much more media reporting and discussion. However, in reality (if not mediated reality), Clinton tweeted three times as often as Trump. From the beginning of the summer campaign season (1 June 2016) to the day before the election (7 November), the substantive tweets (excluding retweets of other people's messages, ceremonial messages such as congratulations to other politicians, and those that were purely organizational such as announcing campaign rallies) by the two candidates combined numbered 4132 (1099 by Trump and 3033 by Clinton). Regardless of impressions created by media reports, Trump did *not* out-tweet Clinton, but quite the reverse. However, their rates of retweeting were similar: the average number of retweets of Clinton's top 100 messages was 27,619 and Trump's average was 29,262. While their degree of retweeting is similar, their content is distinctly different, as illustrated in Table 2.1.

The distinction between Clinton and Trump in regard to threat and oppression is stark. Trump invoked the simple and inciting aspect of cultural conservatism—threat—in 22% of his most popular tweets (many of the others were taken up with insults to Clinton):

Table 2.1 Ideology on Twitter (%)

	Threat	Oppression	Economy	FP/terrorism	Negative
Trump	22***	0***	0**	19***	71
Clinton	2	41	6	4	62

Entries represent the percentage of each candidate's top 100 substantive tweets that invoke a threat, oppression of a social group, the economy, foreign policy or terrorism, or a negative attack on the opposing candidate
*$p < 0.05$; **$p < 0.01$; ***$p < 0.001$

Is President Obama going to finally mention the words radical Islamic terrorism' If he doesn't he should immediately resign in disgrace!

We are TRYING to fight ISIS, and now our own people are killing our police. Our country is divided and out of control. The world is watching

Praying for the families of the two Iowa police who were ambushed this morning. An attack on those who keep us safe is an attack on us all.

Horrific incident in FL. Praying for all the victims & their families. When will this stop? When will we get tough, smart & vigilant

What has happened in Orlando is just the beginning. Our leadership is weak and ineffective. I called it and asked for the ban. Must be tough.

Clinton, on the other hand, focused on pointing out examples of oppression (41% of her tweets):

Donald Trump called her "Miss Piggy" and "Miss Housekeeping." Her name is Alicia Machado. #DebateNight

"I will be a president for all of the people."—Donald Trump* *Except women, people of color, LGBT people, Muslims... #Debate

Alton Sterling Matters. Philando Castile Matters. Black Lives Matter.

LGBT kids are perfect exactly the way they are. #BornPerfect

When Donald Trump speaks about women, our daughters can hear him.

While social justice can apply to poverty, race, ethnicity, gender, sexual orientation, religion, or other identities, different progressive politicians emphasize different concerns. We suggested above that Clinton is more of a multiculturalist (the source of oppression is identity) than a traditional liberal (the source of oppression is poverty). This is borne out in the pattern of her tweets that invoke social justice[10]:

Poor	5%
Muslim	12%
Hispanic	15%
LGBT	15%
Black	29%
Female	59%

When we look at the more complex issue domains for each ideology (the economy for conservatives and foreign policy for liberals), the opposite pattern emerges. Regardless of Trump's emphasis on jobs and trade when he communicates through traditional campaign avenues, over Twitter his mention of the economy was negligible. Clinton invokes the economy more than Trump does, a surprising finding given their campaign themes. When it comes to foreign policy or terrorism, Trump tweets about this topic frequently in simple and inciting terms (19%, compared to Clinton's 4%). As predicted, both sides emphasize negative attacks (71% to 62%, a non-statistically significant difference).

IDEOLOGY AND CITIZEN ENGAGEMENT

One of the goals of political tweeting is to inspire retweeting. So far we have examined Clinton and Trump's most popular tweets. But what makes them more likely to gain attention and be retweeted, spreading the message? In order to test our supposition that the brief and inciting facets of each ideology will be more effective, we compare the top 100 tweets with the next hundred that follow. The results are displayed in Table 2.2.

Trump's top 100 tweets were retweeted on average 29,262 times, while his next most popular 100 were retweeted about half as much, at 17,204. Clinton's tweets followed a similar pattern, with the top 100 receiving on average 27,619 retweets and the next 100 only 9400. What accounts for

Table 2.2   Tweet effectiveness (%)

	Threat	Oppression	Economy	FP/terrorism	Negative
Trump					
Top 100 (average retweets 29,262)	22*	0**	0**	19*	71**
101–200 (average retweets 17,204)***	12	7	8	10	52
Clinton					
Top 100 (average retweets 27,619)	2	41	6	4**	62
101–200 (average retweets 9400)***	3	37	4	15	64

Comparisons of the top 100 most retweeted messages and the 101st—200th most retweeted messages
*$p < 0.05$; **$p < 0.01$; ***$p < 0.001$

these highly statistically significant differences in attention garnered by the brief messages? In Trump's case, there are also statistically significant differences in the invocation of threat, reference to foreign policy or terrorism, and negativity. The brief and provoking aspects of the conservative message—especially threat—are associated with greater retweeting.

Clinton, however, does not show the same pattern. Her invocation of oppression remained constant in her top 200 tweets, with no distinction between those that garner 27,000 or 9000 retweets. The focus on specific oppressed groups also remained the same (women most frequently [41%], followed by Blacks [29%], Muslims [19%], LGBT [16%], Hispanics [14%], and finally the poor [3%]). Clinton's negative attacks on Trump are also at the same pace. While Clinton's tweets contain the elements we hypothesized, they do not seem to be the keys to greater retweeting, but instead characterize the whole of her Twitter campaign.

CONCLUSION

Twitter has moved from a new and uncertain aspect of political campaigns to an established and undeniable force after the 2016 race. Among the questions that remain are which party will benefit more. Prior to this presidential contest, observers could have expected the younger and more social media savvy base of the Democratic Party to have the stronger Twitter presence. Donald Trump's unexpected exploitation of the medium raises the question of how ideology and Twitter intersect.

We argue that Twitter encourages the simple and inciting aspects of each ideology. For Trump's cultural conservatism, that is the invocation of threats to security, to jobs, or to group status. For Clinton's multicultural liberalism, that is the identification of oppression of minority groups. Our analysis of the 2016 tweets indicates that each candidate employed their comparative advantage, and Trump's followers retweeted these appeals at a higher rate, suggesting that these simple and inciting appeals are indeed effective.

Neither ideology is definitively advantaged by Twitter; each can communicate a part of their ideology clearly. To the extent that future candidates on either side focus their Twitter strategy on the specific ideological arguments that fit the Twitter format, they can employ the medium effectively. Less can indeed be more ideological and 140 characters can be a liberating limit.

NOTES

1. On Democratic social media savvy, see Lee and Lim (2016), *The Washington Post* 29 September 2014, "Twitter is for Liberals, Pinterest is for Conservatives." On "shadowbanning" and conservative complaints about censorship, see Bokhari (2016), Sobieski (2017), and Young (2016).
2. Generalizing from a case in the Netherlands, Kessel and Castelein (2016) argue that "the format of tweets—which are limited to 140 characters— arguably offers more opportunities for politicians with a succinct and unambiguous message than for mainstream politicians whose positions are marked by more nuance and opacity" (596).
3. On the propensity for negative attacks on Twitter—which seem correlated with negative campaign strategies in other media and to prolific tweeting— see Bode et al. (2016).
4. Striving for attention may lead to the potential trade-off between authenticity and error. Tweeting in an unfiltered voice may be perceived as authentic and therefore trustworthy (see Lee and Lim 2016: "Trump's unprecedented bold and controversial communication style, which was often framed as 'authenticity,' was clearly differentiated from Clinton's traditional, and thus more predictable, communication style" (854)). The same tactic may lead to errors of judgment that hurt the candidate. Sometimes it is not easy to tell which has occurred. Four months into his presidency, Trump famously tweeted, "Despite the constant negative press covfefe" without further explanation. The next morning, he tweeted: "Who can figure out the true meaning of 'covfefe'??? Enjoy!" When asked at the next press briefing, White House Press Secretary Sean Spicer said, "The President and a small group of people know exactly what he meant." Spicer may or may not have been in that group. Perhaps it was in fact an inside joke. Or an error. We may never know. Did this make him look foolish or more like ordinary people who make authentic mistakes (the "have a beer" heuristic)?
5. See Bode et al. (2016) on the successful generation of free media through reporting on tweets.
6. Ideology is a contested concept, but mainstream political science generally understands it as a vision of a better society, grounded in a constellation of value predispositions and factual perceptions. See Marietta (2011) for a full discussion of the competing foundations of contemporary conservatism and liberalism.
7. See Conway et al. (2015, 2016). Contra earlier arguments summarized by Jost et al. (2003), when we account for differences in domains, each ideology is complex in some areas and simple in others, as predicted by Tetlock (1986).

8. LBJ invoked the threat of nuclear war (see the infamous "Daisy Girl" ad against Goldwater); Reagan invoked the threat from the Soviets (see his "Bear in the Woods" ad); George H.W. Bush invoked the threats of race and crime (see the infamous Willie Horton and "Revolving Door" ads); George W. Bush invoked the threat of terrorism (see the "Wolves" ad); and Hillary Clinton employed the Daisy Girl actor, now in her 50s, to accuse Trump of creating a current danger of nuclear war, but none have run the full spectrum of personal security, personal status, and group status threats as repeatedly and as bluntly as Trump.

9. The tweets for the entire 2016 campaign have been collected and made available by the scholars at Syracuse University School of Information Studies at illuminating.ischool.syr.edu.

10. These categories add up to more than 100% because Clinton sometimes invoked more than one identity group in the same tweet.

REFERENCES

Albertson, Bethany, and Shana Kushner Gadarian. 2015. *Anxious Politics: Democratic Citizenship in a Threatening World*. New York: Cambridge University Press.

Barker, David C. 2002. *Rushed to Judgment: Talk Radio, Persuasion, and American Political Behavior*. New York: Columbia University Press.

Bobo, Lawrence. 1983. Whites' Opposition to Busing: Symbolic Racism or Realistic Group Conflict? *Journal of Personality and Social Psychology* 45 (6): 1196–1210.

Bode, Leticia, David Lassen, Young Mie Kim, Dhavan Shah, Erika Fowler, Travis Ridout, and Michael Franz. 2016. Coherent Campaigns? Campaign Broadcast and Social Messaging. *Online Information Review* 40 (5): 580–594.

Bokhari, Allum. 2016. Conservative Twitter Users Should Fight Back. *Breitbart*, February 17.

Boyer, Pascal, and Nora Parren. 2015. Threat-Related Information Suggests Competence: A Possible Factor in the Spread of Rumors. *PloS One* 10 (6): e0128421.

Conway, Lucien, Laura Gornick, Shannon Houck, Christopher Anderson, Jennifer Stockert, Diana Sessoms, and Kevin McCue. 2015. Are Conservatives Really More Simple-Minded Than Liberals? The Domain Specificity of Complex Thinking. *Political Psychology* 37 (6): 777–798.

Conway, Lucien, Shannon Houck, Laura Gornick, and Meredith Repke. 2016. Ideologically Motivated Perceptions of Complexity: Believing Those Who Agree with You Are More Complex Than They Are. *Journal of Language and Social Psychology* 35 (6): 708–718.

Feldman, Stanley, and Karen Stenner. 1997. Perceived Threat and Authoritarianism. *Political Psychology* 18 (4): 741–770.

Gadarian, Shana Kushner. 2010. The Politics of Threat: How Terrorism News Shapes Foreign Policy Attitudes. *Journal of Politics* 72 (2): 469–483.

Gross, Justin, and Kaylee Johnson. 2016. Twitter Taunts and Tirades: Negative Campaigning in the Age of Trump. *PS: Political Science & Politics* 49 (4): 748–754.

Jost, Jon, J. Glaser, A. Kruglanski, and F. Sulloway. 2003. Political Conservatism as Motivated Social Cognition. *Psychological Bulletin* 129 (3): 339–375.

Kessel, Stinj, and Remco Castelein. 2016. Shifting the Blame: Populist Politicians' Use of Twitter as a Tool of Opposition. *Journal of Contemporary European Research* 12 (2): 594–614.

Landau, Mark, Sheldon Solomon, Jeff Greenberg, et al. 2004. Deliver Us From Evil: The Effects of Mortality Salience and Reminders of 9/11 on Support for President George W. Bush. *Personality and Social Psychology Bulletin* 30 (9): 1135–1150.

Lee, Jayeon, and Young-Shin Lim. 2016. Gendered Campaign Tweets: The Cases of Hillary Clinton and Donald Trump. *Public Relations Review* 42 (5): 849–855.

Marietta, Morgan. 2011. *A Citizen's Guide to American Ideology: Conservatism and Liberalism in Contemporary Politics.* New York: Routledge.

Merolla, Jennifer, and Elizabeth Zechmeister. 2013. Evaluating Political Leaders in Times of Terror and Economic Threat: The Conditioning Influence of Political Partisanship. *Journal of Politics* 75 (3): 599–612.

Onreat, Emma, Alain van Hiel, and Ilse Cornelius. 2013. Threat and Right-Wing Attitude: A Cross-National Approach. *Political Psychology* 34 (5): 791.

Petriglieri, Jennifer. 2011. Under Threat: Responses to and the Consequences of Threats to Individuals' Identities. *Academy of Management Review* 36 (4): 641–662.

Petrocik, John. 1996. Issue Ownership in Presidential Elections, with a 1980 Case Study. *American Journal of Political Science* 40: 825–850.

Pyszczynski, Thomas, Sheldon Solomon, and Jeff Greenberg. 2003. *In the Wake of 9/11: The Psychology of Terror.* Washington, DC: American Psychological Association.

Schmid, Katharina, and Orla Muldoon. 2015. Perceived Threat, Social Identification, and Psychological Well-Being: The Effect of Political Conflict Exposure. *Political Psychology* 36 (1): 75–92.

Sobieski, Daniel. 2017. Twitter, Shadowbanning, and Conservatives. *American Thinker*, May 11.

Tetlock, Philip. 1986. A Value Pluralism Model of Ideological Reasoning. *Journal of Personality and Social Psychology* 50: 819–827.

Young, Cathy. 2016. How Facebook, Twitter Silence Conservative Voices Online. *The Hill*, October 28.

CHAPTER 3

Tweet You Very Much: An Analysis of Candidate Twitter Usage from the 2016 Iowa Caucus to Super Tuesday

J. Scott Granberg-Rademacker and Kevin Parsneau

Abstract The 2016 presidential primary featured the widespread use of Twitter by candidates. This chapter examines Twitter use by the two leading candidates from each party (Trump, Cruz, Clinton, and Sanders) from the Iowa Caucus through Super Tuesday. Their strategies reflected scholarly findings as well as unique aspects of their situations. They attacked other primary candidates and the other party, publicized policy positions, promoted campaign organizations, and informed supporters. Trump and Cruz, reflecting their crowded race, aimed more attacks at other Republicans. Meanwhile, Democrats tweeted more about policy and attacked each other less. Clinton's presumptive nominee status and resource advantage allowed her to attack her primary opponent least, focusing instead on attacking Republicans and tweeting information about herself, while Trump, Cruz, and Sanders tried to make up for their relative organizational weaknesses. Clinton's strategy reflected scholars' expectations for incumbents, while the others to some extent reflected the strategies associated with challengers.

J.S. Granberg-Rademacker (✉) • K. Parsneau
Minnesota State University, Mankato, MN, USA

© The Author(s) 2018   21
C.J. Galdieri et al. (eds.), *The Role of Twitter in the 2016 US Election*,
https://doi.org/10.1007/978-3-319-68981-4_3

Keywords Twitter • Candidate image • Presidential election • Earned media

The 2008 presidential campaign has been branded as the defining election cycle for the microblogging site Twitter in terms of messaging and fund-raising (Carr 2008). During the 2008 election, the Obama campaign effectively leveraged social media tools like Twitter to break fund-raising records and mobilize grassroots more successfully than ever before (Tumasjan et al. 2010). President Obama's social media success was noted by congressional candidates in the following 2010 midterm election, where nearly every congressional candidate had an active Twitter account that was actively reaching out to recruit new supporters (Bode and Dalrymple 2016).

Since 2008, Twitter has been increasingly used for a variety of political purposes. Political dissidents utilized Twitter as their primary mode of organizing and spreading their message during the *Arab Spring*, including the 2011 Egyptian revolution that ultimately led to the resignation of President Hosni Mubarak (Salem 2015). Twitter is also increasingly seen by candidates as a way to drive the news cycle and gain the initiative over the media's coverage of events, the candidate's message or campaign (Holtz-Bacha and Zeh 2017). Others have used Twitter to communicate and engage with constituents (Straus et al. 2013), and there is some evidence to suggest that the number of followers one has on social media can be an indicator of electoral success (Williams and Gulati 2008). There is no question that social media, Twitter especially, has become a long-term feature of American politics and indeed politics around the globe.

The question we aim to answer in this chapter is: how did the leading candidates use Twitter during the early part of the 2016 primary campaign season? With the benefit of hindsight, we know that social media tools, like Twitter, were heavily utilized by at least one presidential campaign (Trump and, to a lesser extent, Sanders) in lieu of a traditional campaign "ground game." We also know that journalists' views of social media have changed, to the point where many reporters see Twitter as "the new AP wire" (Molyneux et al. 2017), which could lead to more "free" coverage by traditional media for candidates that use Twitter in attention-grabbing ways.

Twitter as a Campaign Tool

Starting from Mayhew's (1974) premise that elected officials are concerned with reelection and actively seek platforms to publicize information that might further their reelection aims, it logically follows that Twitter would be a highly utilized political tool to that end. Much of the research on campaign use of Twitter has focused on congressional races (for a survey of this research, see Evans and Clark 2016; Evans et al. 2014; Lasson and Brown 2011; Williams and Gulati 2012) with fewer studies focusing on Barack Obama's Twitter campaign in 2008 and 2012 (Bhattacharya et al. 2016; Hamby 2017; Vargo et al. 2014).

Evans et al. (2014) conducted an analysis of the 2012 campaign and found that congressional incumbents and challengers used Twitter in different ways, with the challenger often attempting to leverage Twitter against the incumbency advantage of their opponent. They point out that the challenger's effort to overcome the incumbency advantage manifests itself in a number of different ways on Twitter. First, congressional incumbents tended to have more followers than their challengers, but that challengers tweeted much more often about their campaign. Also, challengers were much more likely to engage in attack tweeting of their opponent. They were also much more likely to tweet about their campaign activities, provide links to media stories, and challengers also tended to be more likely to interact with other users on Twitter and respond to questions or engage in discussions with followers. In short, when facing an opponent with institutional advantages, candidates are more likely to use Twitter as a way to connect with potential supporters and also use Twitter to broadcast their message or attacks on their opponent.

Evidence also shows that demographic differences among the candidates themselves tend to predict how they use Twitter. Evans and Clark (2016) found that women were more likely than men to discuss policy issues and in particular "women's issues." Being younger and being a member of the minority party in Congress also tended to predict increased Twitter use (Straus et al. 2013). In terms of race, Gainous and Wagner (2014) found that white candidates were more likely to tweet attack-style tweets than were African-American or Latino candidates. White candidates were also slightly more likely to tweet about their policy positions on issues.

Candidates are also keenly aware that social media can significantly impact their image. Recently, several scholars have conducted studies, like political sentiment analysis, that link perceptions of candidate image on social media with electoral results. The idea behind political sentiment analysis is to systematically classify the sentiment of political tweets about candidates in an effort to predict electoral results based on the sentiments expressed in these tweets. These studies have had mixed success in predicting electoral outcomes. Gayo-Avello et al. (2011) found sentiment analysis to be a poor predictor of a 2010 special congressional election in Massachusetts. Mejova et al. (2013) conducted sentiment analysis on GOP Presidential candidates from January 2011 to January 2012 and found little connection between political chatter on Twitter and national poll numbers. However, Marchetti-Bowick and Chambers (2012) found that sentiment analysis on Twitter can be used to accurately track Gallup's Presidential Job Approval poll results. Bhattacharya et al. (2016) expanded traditional sentiment analysis to examine how personal adjectives (brave, intelligent, cool, etc.) of Obama and Romney in the 2012 election and found this to be a considerable improvement in electoral prediction as well as tracking political sentiment on social media with national polls. Despite the mixed empirical evidence, candidates pay attention to their social media image because one's impression on social media can reflect in the polls on election day.

Candidates also use Twitter for different reasons. One of the main reasons for candidates to use Twitter is to broadcast information in one direction—from the candidate to the public. There is convincing evidence to suggest that this is one of the main reasons why candidates and elected officials use Twitter (Golbeck et al. 2010; Hemphill et al. 2013; Small 2010). Even though Hemphill et al. (2013) found that sitting members of Congress do not generally use Twitter to ask followers to take action, content analysis conducted by Parmelee and Bichard (2012) of tweets from 12 congressional races in 2010 found that candidates who are running for election or reelection use Twitter in a much different way during the campaign season. They found that candidates used Twitter as a platform to attack their opponents and as a way to mobilize action from their followers. Candidates (especially challengers) also used Twitter to inform followers about campaign events. Furthermore, they found varying degrees of interaction between candidates and their followers, suggesting that some candidates were engaged in political conversations with their followers.

The above theoretical discussion suggests a set of expectations about how 2016 presidential primary candidates would use social media like Twitter. Given her status as the dominant, presumptive nominee, we expect that Clinton would behave similar to incumbents, while Trump, Cruz, and Sanders display the patterns of challengers. Scholars have found that challengers tweet more than incumbents so we expect more tweets from Trump, Cruz, and Sanders than Clinton. We also expect Clinton to make fewer attacks on her primary opponent, with other candidates engaging in more attacks. Her advantage in campaign resources should also mean that she had less need to use Twitter for organizational purposes.

Some unique aspects of the 2016 primary create other expectations about candidates' Twitter use. While Martin O'Malley was still technically in the race in early 2016, he was not realistically competitive. We expect the two-candidate race on the Democratic side to mean that Clinton and Sanders had greater incentives to act like they would be in the general election. Both should attack the opposition party and its candidates more, to demonstrate their general election strength to undecided Democrats, and both have fewer incentive to attack the other and potentially offend those supporters, and, thus, we expect them to tweet more about policy and general information. Meanwhile, Trump and Cruz competed with a crowded field of 14 other Republican candidates and have incentives to attack other Republicans to win the competition. Furthermore, there are also logical strategic times for all candidates to use Twitter. It makes sense that candidates would marshal tweets in their organization efforts around the Iowa Caucus, New Hampshire primary, and Super Tuesday competitions. Similarly, we expect different uses of Twitter around the scheduled debates.

DATA AND METHODS

Candidate tweets were gathered using the Twitter API for a time period of 32 days before the 2016 Iowa Caucus (January 30, 2016) through Super Tuesday (March 1, 2016). To determine which candidates to collect tweets from, we took the two top candidates placing in the Iowa Caucus from each party: Donald Trump and Ted Cruz for the Republicans and Hillary Clinton and Bernie Sanders for the Democrats. Each of these candidates were also the most competitive in their respective presidential primaries for the longest duration. In addition to tweets, we collected the time and day stamp of the tweet and the number of retweets each candidate's tweet had—we used this as a measure of support for the content of the tweet and association with the candidate (Tsugawa and Kito 2017).

Using Twitter's API, we scraped 254 tweets from Donald Trump's official Twitter account, @realDonaldTrump, during the 32 days of our study. We obtained 268 tweets from Ted Cruz in a similar fashion, through his two official Twitter accounts, @tedcruz and @SenTedCruz. During this same time period, we collected 281 tweets from Hillary Clinton's official Twitter account, @HillaryClinton, and we collected 391 tweets from Bernie Sanders' two official Twitter accounts, @BernieSanders and @SenSanders. In total, there were $N=1194$ tweets.

We used a modified version of Gainous and Wagner's (2014) tweet classifications. They used four different categories to classify tweets: informational, organizational, policy, and attack/negative campaigning. Informational tweets are tweets that say something about the candidate as a person, like an adherence to certain ideological principles, being hardworking, having a strong faith, and so on. Organizational tweets are tweets with information about campaign events, calls for volunteers, asking people to get out and vote, and so on. Policy tweets are tweets that allow the reader to glean some information about where the candidate stands on a given policy issue, like immigration, health care, the deficit, and so on. Attack/negative campaigning tweets are tweets that sling mud, ridicule, or go after an opponent in an aggressive way. Like others (Evans et al. 2014), we modified the attack/negative campaigning category because we wanted to track specifically who or what each candidate was attacking in an effort to find out if attack tweets targets were different across the candidates. We segmented this category into five different sub-categories: (1) attack candidate from the same party, (2) attack the other party or other party candidates, (3) attack one's own party, (4) attack the media, and (5) attack the wealthy or "special interests." Table 3.1 shows examples of the different types of tweets for each category.

To code the tweets, both authors were assigned two-thirds of all the tweets for each candidate, with one-third of the tweets being assigned to both authors. The authors then coded each of the tweets into the aforementioned categories (it was possible for tweets to be coded into more than one category). The codings from both authors were then compared against one another, and it was found that they agreed on 94.5% of all tweet classifications. The authors then reconciled all of the classification differences on a case-by-case basis.

DISCUSSION

Previous scholarship argues that officeholders and candidates use Twitter for strategic purposes and analysis indicates that 2016 presidential primary candidates also did so between January 30 and March 1, 2016. Overall, both Democratic candidates tweeted more than the Republicans between

Table 3.1 Examples of tweet types

Tweet category	Tweeter/tweet
Attack candidate	@realDonaldTrump: Lightweight Marco Rubio was working hard last night. The problem is, he is a choker, and once a choker, always a choker! Mr. Meltdown
Attack other party	@HillaryClinton: In Ohio and across the country, Republicans are once again attacking women's health. We won't stand for this. http://hrc.io/1PTP6Wh
Attack own party	@BernieSanders: It's hard to be a real progressive and take on the establishment when you've become dependent on Wall St. and drug company money. #DemDebate
Attack media	@realDonaldTrump: @FoxNews is so biased it is disgusting. They do not want Trump to win. All negative!
Attack wealthy/special interests	@BernieSanders: A handful of people on Wall Street have extraordinary power. In 2008, their illegal behavior nearly destroyed the U.S. and global economy
Organizational	@tedcruz: Get ready to cast your ballot on #SuperTuesday. Commit to #ChooseCruz: https://www.tedcruz.org/super-tuesday/pic.twitter.com/qfemq1NsnH
Informational	@tedcruz: As president, I will stand firm with the American people, whether Washington likes it or not! https://amp.twimg.com/v/5bc9d3b3-efb4-45e6-95d2-a7fba5db0d6c???
Policy	@HillaryClinton: Too many kids are being criminalized instead of educated. Here's how we will end the school-to-prison pipeline: http://hrc.io/1Ww20eS

Source: Twitter.com

January 31 and March 1, with Sanders clearly leading in volume with 391 tweets compared to Clinton's 281 tweets. Cruz tweeted 268 times, and, despite the attention surrounding his Twitter account, Trump tweeted the least with 254 tweets. Lacking traditional campaign resources, Trump relied more heavily on social media resources like Twitter particularly to attack primary opponents and his own party. Other candidates used their Twitter accounts more to make policy statements, promote their organizational efforts, or provide informational tweets.

While all four candidates tweeted attacks against their primary opponents, Trump's 87 tweets (Fig. 3.1), criticizing mostly Cruz, Rubio, and Bush, represent more primary opponent attacks than Cruz, Clinton, and Sanders combined. Despite fewer tweets, Republicans attacked their primary opponents more than Democrats, with Cruz attacking 36 times, while Sanders attacked 29 times and Clinton 17 times. These strategies may

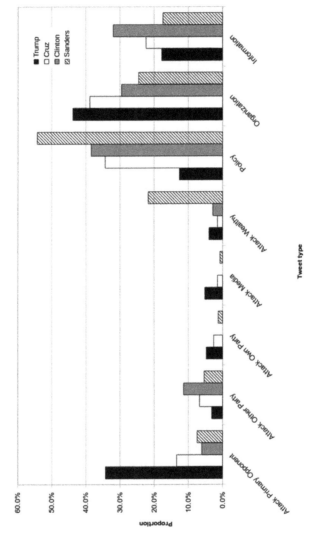

Fig. 3.1 Proportion of tweets by category for all four candidates

reflect the large number of Republicans competing, but Clinton's few attacks also suggest that as the presumptive nominee she was cautious and hoping to woo Sanders's voters for the general election. Trump led with 12 tweets criticizing the Republican Party, but Cruz also tried to position himself as an outsider with 7 attacks on his party. Meanwhile, Sanders attacked the Democratic Party five times, while Clinton did not criticize her party, as might be expected from a presumptive nominee.

On the other hand, Clinton made more attacks on the other party, with 32 tweets, which is more than the other three candidates in the study. She appears to have been positioning herself for the general election, while Sanders tweeted 21 times demonstrating his ability to criticize Republicans. Democrats made more attacks on Republicans and their party, while Trump and Cruz fought each other and other Republicans, with 12 and 7 tweets, respectively. The main targets of Sanders's attacks were the wealthy and corporations as his 85 tweets far outnumber the others' tweets, with Trump's 10, Clinton's 8, and Cruz's 4 attacks on the wealthy. Meanwhile, Trump complained about the media more than other three candidates, with 13 tweets compared to Cruz's 4 tweets, Sanders's 3, and none by Clinton.

Candidates used Twitter for other purposes, too. Sanders positioned himself as a Democratic Socialist to the left of Clinton and tweeted an enormous 212 times informing followers of his liberal policy positions as central to his appeal. The Democratic competition was more focused on policy, as Clinton made 108 policy tweets. Cruz made 92 policy tweets and Trump made only 32 policy tweets, displaying his lack of interest in policy issues. Democrats also led in informational tweets, with Clinton's 90 tweets reflecting efforts to rebrand herself among Democratic activists and Sanders tweeting 68 informational tweets, while Cruz sent 60 informational tweets and Trump sent only 45.

All four candidates used Twitter to generate organizational support for events, rallies, and get-out-the-vote efforts. Trump lacked grassroots activism and campaign staff support and relied most heavily on free media, including social media like Twitter with the highest number of organizational tweets at 111 tweets. Cruz, also involved in the crowded Republican field, was a close second with 104 tweets, while Sanders made organizational 96 tweets and Clinton with the strongest traditional campaign made 83 tweets. Clinton's fewer organizational tweets reflect her similarity with the expectations for incumbent candidates whose campaign strength reduces the need to use social media for traditional campaign activities. The overall impression from Table 3.1 is that Trump used Twitter as a tool for attacking opponents and creating an informal campaign, while the other three focused more on policy, Cruz attacked opponents in a crowded primary, Sanders positioned himself to left of the presumptive nominee, and Clinton tweeted with an eye toward the general election.

While tweets reflect candidates' efforts, retweets reflect the enthusiasm of their followers for their message. One clear conclusion from the data is that Sanders and Trump dominated in social media enthusiasm in the form of retweets. Both had over a million retweets during this period, with Sanders tweeting more times to get more retweets (1.04 million) compared to Trump (1.03 million). Meanwhile, Clinton's followers retweeted her 0.38 million times and Cruz's followers retweeted him 0.20 million times. Trump's supporters magnified his message more than any of the candidates as they retweeted him at an average of 4054 per tweet (Fig. 3.2). Sanders's followers were second with an average 2657 retweets per tweet. Clinton's followers were a distant third with 1354 retweets per tweet and Cruz's followers fourth with only 738 retweets per tweet. Sanders and Trump demonstrated a great deal of online enthusiasm.

While the candidates tweeted attacks against their competition for the party nomination, most followers were more enthusiastic about attacks on the other party. Trump's attacks on his primary opponents were retweeted a lot, on average 3741 retweets each, but his attacks on Democrats averaged 5123 retweets. Sanders's attacks on Republicans averaged 5727 retweets, while his attacks on Clinton were retweeted only 2590 on average. Clinton's attacks against Republicans averaged 1667 retweets, while she was only retweeted on average 1278 times when she targeted Sanders. Only Cruz's attacks on other Republicans, usually Trump, had a significantly higher average (1375) than his average tweet or attacks on the other party (873). Cruz generated less enthusiasm on Twitter, but compared to the followers of Trump, Sanders, or Clinton, his followers were significantly focused on beating his primary opponents relative to his average retweets. These findings may reflect Cruz's struggle for attention among the many non-Trump Republicans.

While there are fewer average retweets for each candidate, retweets of attacks on the candidates' party follow the same pattern as retweets of attacks on the opposition party. Trump created the greatest enthusiasm with 51,277 retweets of his attacks on the Republican Party, with an average of 4273 retweets per tweet. Sanders tweets against the Democratic Party were retweeted 27,130 times, with an average of 5426 retweets per tweet. Cruz's followers retweeted him 5821 times, with an average of 832 per

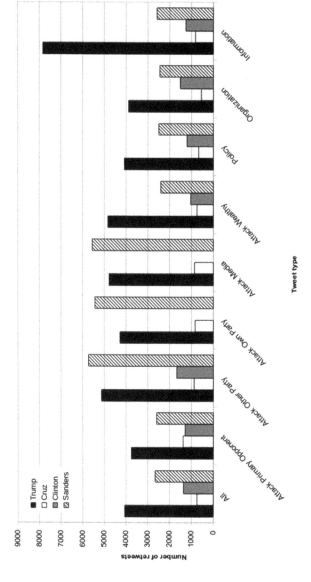

Fig. 3.2 Number of retweets by category for all four candidates

tweet. Clinton did not attack her own party. While this finding should be taken with caution given the few tweets and the numbers of retweets were not significantly different from candidates' averages, the general enthusiasm about retweeting attacks on either party demonstrates overall distrust of the major parties among followers of the three candidates. Clinton's followers were enthusiastic about attacks on Republicans, but we do not have an indicator of their willingness to retweet complaints about her party because Clinton abstained from tweeting it.

A few other observations stand out from the analysis of retweets in Fig. 3.2. Attacks on the media were also popular retweets among supporters of Sanders with 5553 average retweets. Trump and Cruz were retweeted 4780 and 863 times, respectively. However, despite the enthusiasm generated by these tweets and the media attention they received, these tweets represent a small fraction of the overall tweets, and only Sanders's tweets were retweeted significantly more than his average tweet. Trump seemed to get the most attention among pundits from these attacks, but only made 13 tweets, or 5.1% of all his tweets, attacking the media. Meanwhile, only 0.8% of Sanders's tweets and of 1.5% Cruz's tweets criticized the media. Clinton did not tweet an attack the media during this time period. Clinton's actions match our expectations that she would act similar to incumbents and resist the temptation to attack either her party or the media, while the other candidates act more like challengers.

Sanders made economic inequality a campaign focus and used social media to deliver that message. He made 85 tweets (21.7%) attacking the wealthy. However, these attacks were retweeted significantly less (2407) than his average tweet. They did not generate as much enthusiasm. Clinton experienced similar reactions among her followers, with significantly fewer retweets of her attacks on wealthy (1036) compared to her average tweet. Only Trump, with 3.9% of his tweets attacking the wealthy, averaged more retweets (4832) for an attack on the wealthy than his average tweet, although the difference was not statistically significant. Trump's common assertion in these tweets was that his own wealth frees him from the influence of wealthy interests, and he attracted followers critical of the upper class. In fact, Trump's tweets attacking the wealthy were retweeted on average more than Sanders's attacks on the wealthy.

The candidates also used Twitter to state their policy positions in 140 characters or less. As shown on Fig. 3.2, these tweets were large proportions of candidate tweets but received less retweeting in general than attack tweets. Sanders (54.2%), Clinton (38.4%), and Cruz (34.3%) tweeted relatively frequently and about policy positions, and for Clinton and Cruz these tweets were retweeted fewer times (1210 and 670, respectively) than their average tweets. Only Trump, frequently criticized for his disinterest in policy, averaged more retweets (4078) for policy tweets than his overall average, although this difference total was not statistically significant.

Candidates also tweeted to promote their campaign organization and activities. For Trump, Clinton, and Sanders, organizational tweets averaged fewer retweets than candidates' retweets' overall averages. Cruz's followers were significantly less likely ($p = 0.000$) to retweet his organizational tweets urging them to events or to go to the polls. Despite Trump's efforts to replicate a campaign organization with social media and celebrity status, his organizational retweets did not generate significantly more retweets than his average. Overall, these findings may reflect that the events and elections were in particular states while the Twitter followers were nationwide. It makes little sense for a follower in another state to retweet about campaign events in Iowa or a reminder to vote in New Hampshire if they do not have any followers near those places.

Twitter is a means for candidates to provide followers information about themselves. These efforts represented a substantial portion of the candidates' tweets, but were not significantly magnified by their followers. Informational retweets by the Democrats, Clinton and Sanders, were retweeted less than their average tweets, at 1257 and 2584, respectively. On the other hand, informational tweets by Trump and Cruz were retweeted more than their overall averages, at 7830 and 819, respectively. Although Trump's average retweet was particularly high, it is driven by a few popular outlier tweets, and the numbers of retweets for informational tweets were not significantly different from the averages for any candidate at the $p < 0.05$ level.

Among the most important primary candidate uses for Twitter are attacks on primary opponents and the opposite party and its candidates. Tweets criticizing primary opponents strategically position a candidate to win the nomination, and Fig. 3.3 reports tweets attacking primary opponents over time. It shows candidates acting according to scholarly expectations in the context of this race. Trump and Cruz attacked each other and other Republican candidates, primarily Bush and Rubio, more at times around the debates and elections. Clinton and Sanders largely abstained from attacking each other, except around debates when they met face to face. While the two Republicans in a crowded field ramped up attacks around primaries and caucuses, the Democrats appear to have preferred to

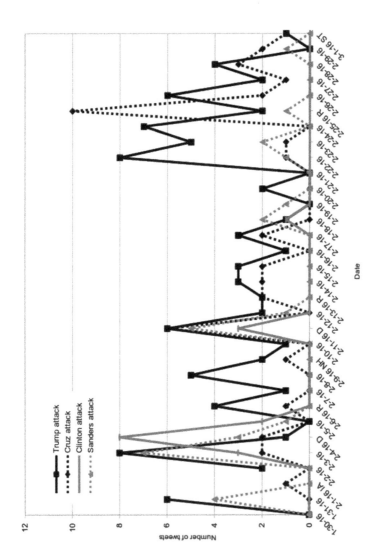

Fig. 3.3 Tweets attacking primary opponents by all four candidates, over time. The Iowa Caucus is denoted with "IA" next to 2-1-16, the New Hampshire primary is denoted with "NH" next to 2-9-16, and Super Tuesday is denoted with "ST" next to 3-1-16. Dates of Republican debates are denoted with an "R" next to the date and dates of Democratic debates are denoted with a "D" next to the date

minimize intra-party conflict. This finding supports the expectation that Democrats, with essentially only two candidates in the competition, would attack each other fewer times.

Figure 3.4 graphs attacks on the opposing party and candidates over time and also reveals differences between the Democrats compared to the Republicans in a crowded field. Clinton, presumably with an eye toward the general election, used the opportunities of Republican debates to attack them and their party, while Sanders also attacked Republicans, although fewer times. Meanwhile, Trump made a few, regular attacks against the Democrats, but there was no consistent pattern relative to any particular events. Cruz focused on his primary opponents rather than Democrats, although he used the occasions of Republican debates to make additional attacks against Democrats. Examining the two types of attacks, it is noteworthy that both slow down just before and on Super Tuesday, suggesting that its intense schedule taxes candidates' time even to tweet.

Figures 3.5, 3.6, and 3.7 graph policy, organizational, and informational tweets for the candidates over time. Sanders and Clinton (Fig. 3.5) had the largest proportions of policy tweets and both consistently tweeted about their policy positions throughout the competition, especially around Democratic debates, with Sanders consistently tweeting policy positions more often. Cruz also tweeted about policy throughout the competition, and more around Republican debates, while Trump had few policy tweets. On the other hand, Trump (Fig. 3.6) had the largest proportion of organizational tweets and consistently sent them, with more activity around the primary and caucus dates as would be expected. Clinton and Sanders used organizational tweets with greater frequency just before and during the three competitions. Cruz also sent organizational tweets around the Iowa Caucus and New Hampshire primary, but sent out only a couple organizational tweets per day leading up to Super Tuesday. Clinton (Fig. 3.7) tweeted the most informational tweets, and she, Sanders, and Cruz consistently sent them throughout the competition. Trump sent few informational tweets prior to the Republican debate on February 25, but markedly increased the number after it.

Figure 3.8 graphs retweets of the candidates over time, and the main impression from it is that Trump and Sanders consistently dominated Cruz and Clinton in retweets. Also, while candidates might hope to increase enthusiasm among their followers at strategic points in the competition, the data indicates that each candidate experienced fairly consistent levels of retweets, interspersed with a few resonating tweets that generated a many retweets. For the most part, there is evidence that the type of tweet in

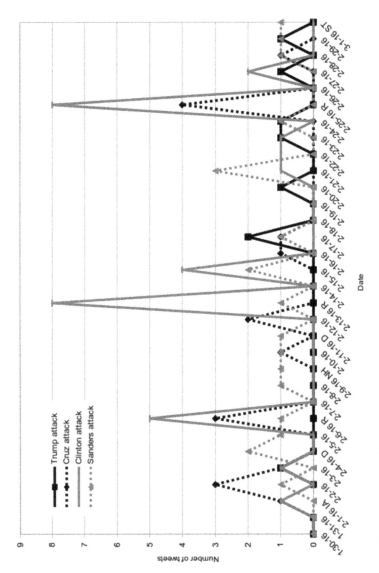

Fig. 3.4 Tweets attacking the opposite party and candidates by all four candidates, over time. The Iowa Caucus is denoted with "IA" next to 2-1-16, the New Hampshire primary is denoted with "NH" next to 2-9-16, and Super Tuesday is denoted with "ST" next to 3-1-16. Dates of Republican debates are denoted with an "R" next to the date and dates of Democratic debates are denoted with a "D" next to the date

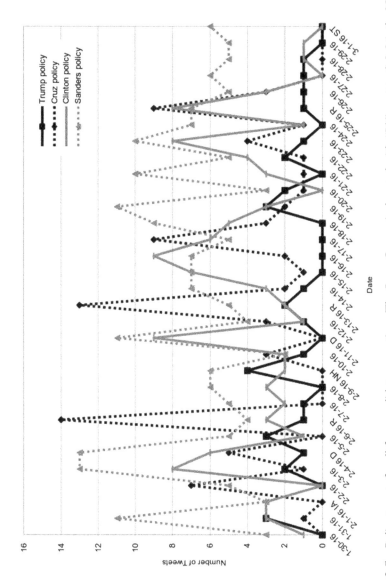

Fig. 3.5 Policy tweets for all four candidates over time. The Iowa Caucus is denoted with "IA" next to 2-1-16, the New Hampshire primary is denoted with "NH" next to 2-9-16, and Super Tuesday is denoted with "ST" next to 3-1-16. Dates of Republican debates are denoted with an "R" next to the date and dates of Democratic debates are denoted with a "D" next to the date

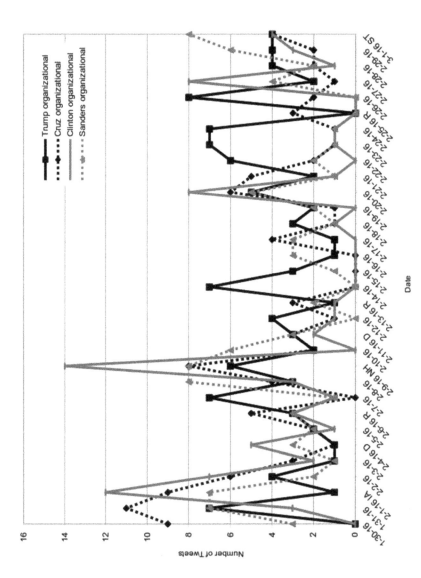

Fig. 3.6 Organizational tweets for all four candidates over time. The Iowa Caucus is denoted with "IA" next to 2-1-16, the New Hampshire primary is denoted with "NH" next to 2-9-16, and Super Tuesday is denoted with "ST" next to 3-1-16. Dates of Republican debates are denoted with an "R" next to the date and dates of Democratic debates are denoted with a "D" next to the date

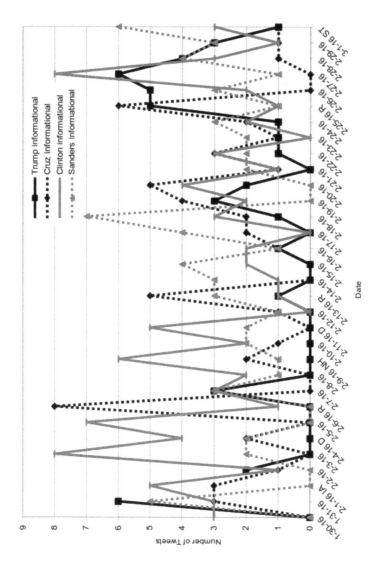

Fig. 3.7 Informational tweets for all four candidates over time. The Iowa Caucus is denoted with "IA" next to 2-1-16, the New Hampshire primary is denoted with "NH" next to 2-9-16, and Super Tuesday is denoted with "ST" next to 3-1-16. Dates of Republican debates are denoted with an "R" next to the date and dates of Democratic debates are denoted with a "D" next to the date

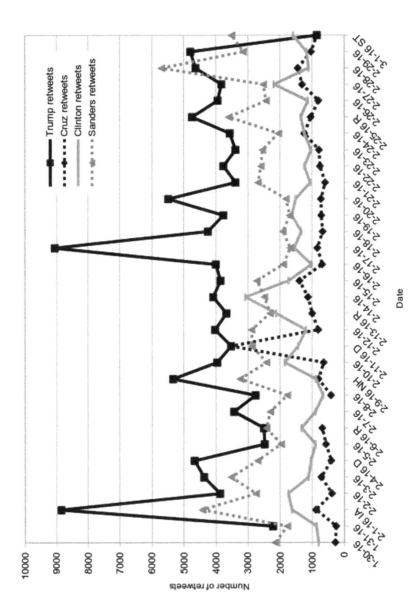

Fig. 3.8 Total retweets for all four candidates over time. The Iowa Caucus is denoted with "IA" next to 2-1-16, the New Hampshire primary is denoted with "NH" next to 2-9-16, and Super Tuesday is denoted with "ST" next to 3-1-16. Dates of Republican debates are denoted with an "R" next to the date and dates of Democratic debates are denoted with a "D" next to the date

Fig. 3.9 Most retweeted tweets for all four candidates

general matters, but it does not appear to matter when candidates tweet or whether activity would be to their advantage. Some tweets just resonate among followers and get retweeted.

We examined the individual tweets. Figure 3.9 shows the most popular tweets of each candidate with an additional tweet by Trump. Among this sample, Sanders had the most retweeted tweet from February 28, supporting President Obama and attacking Trump for refusing to condemn the KKK. Trump's most popular tweet, from February 17, criticized Fox News for bias against him. Clinton's most retweeted message, from February 27, explicitly asked her followers to retweet it, and Cruz's most retweeted tweet, from February 13, commemorated the death of Antonin Scalia. Finally, Trump's most retweeted message prior to the New Hampshire primary was an informational tweet about his campaign being more interesting than the Super Bowl.

CONCLUSIONS

Twitter has become a staple of politics and campaigns and 2016 presidential primary candidates in the early competitions used Twitter in ways that reflected scholar's findings as well as unique aspects of their situations. Trump, Cruz, Clinton, and Sanders attacked other primary candidates, attacked the other party and its candidates, publicized their policy positions, promoted their campaign organization, and provided information to their followers and followers' followers. Clinton, with her strong campaign machine and position as the presumptive nominee, used Twitter in line with scholars' findings about incumbents. She attacked her primary opponent least among the four and focused on tweeting attacks against the Republican Party and her potential opponents in the general election. Reflecting the two-candidate nature of the competition, both Democrats tweeted more about their policy positions than Republicans, and Sanders also resisted attacking Clinton but overall attacked more, to some extent reflecting strategies associated with challengers. Meanwhile, Trump and Cruz, competing among 16 primary candidates, aimed more attacks at other primary candidates. Clinton's resource advantage allowed her to tweet information about herself, while Trump, Cruz, and Sanders used Twitter to make up for their relative organizational weaknesses. In general, candidates tweeted more around debates and the election days, attacking opponents on Twitter they were confronting face to face or ramping up efforts to win the nomination.

REFERENCES

Bhattacharya, Sanmitra, Chao Yang, Padmini Srinivasan, and Bob Boynton. 2016. Perceptions of Presidential Candidates' Personalities in Twitter. *Journal of the Association for Information Science and Technology* 67 (2): 249–267.

Bode, Leticia, and Kajsa Dalrymple. 2016. Politics in 140 Characters or Less: Campaign Communication, Network Interaction, and Political Participation on Twitter. *Journal of Political Marketing* 15: 311–332.

Carr, David. 2008. How Obama Tapped into Social Networks' Power. *The New York Times*, November 9.

Evans, Heather K., and Jennifer H. Clark. 2016. 'You Tweet Like a Girl': How Female Candidates Campaign on Twitter. *American Politics Research* 44 (2): 326–352.

Evans, Heather K., Victoria Cordova, and Savannah Sipole. 2014. Twitter Style: An Analysis of How House Candidates Used Twitter in Their 2012 Campaigns. *PS: Political Science and Politics* 47 (2): 454–462.

Gainous, Jason, and Kevin M. Wagner. 2014. *Tweeting to Power: The Social Media Revolution in American Politics.* New York: Oxford University Press.

Gayo-Avello, Daniel, Panagiotis T. Metaxas, and Eni Mustafaraj. 2011. Limits on Electoral Predictions Using Twitter. In *Proceedings of the Fifth International AAAI Conference on Weblogs and Social Media*, 490–493. Barcelona.

Golbeck, Jennifer, Justin Grimes, and Anthony Rogers. 2010. Twitter Use by the U.S. Congress. *Journal of the American Society for Information Science and Technology* 61 (8): 1612–1621.

Hamby, Peter. 2017. Did Twitter Kill the Boys on the Bus? A Report from the Romney Campaign in 2012. In *Twitter and Elections Around the World: Campaigns in 140 Characters or Less*, ed. Richard Davis, Christina Holtz-Bacha, and Marion R. Just, 13–26. New York: Routledge.

Hemphill, Libby, Jahna Otterbacher, and Matthew A. Shapiro. 2013. What's Congress Doing on Twitter? In *Proceedings of the 2013 Conference on Computer Supported Cooperative Work*, 877–886. San Antonio.

Holtz-Bacha, Christina, and Reimar Zeh. 2017. Tweeting to the Press? Effects of Political Twitter Activity on Offline Media in the 2013 German Election Campaign. In *Twitter and Elections Around the World: Campaigns in 140 Characters or Less*, ed. Richard Davis, Christina Holtz-Bacha, and Marion R. Just, 27–42. New York: Routledge.

Lassen, David S., and Adam R. Brown. 2011. Twitter: The Electoral Connection? *Social Science Computer Review* 29 (4): 419–436.

Marchetti-Bowick, Micol, and Nathanael Chambers. 2012. Learning for Microblogs with Distant Supervision: Political Forecasting with Twitter. In *Proceedings of the 13th Conference of the European Chapter of the Association of Computational Linguistics*, 603–612. Avignon.

Mayhew, David. 1974. *Congress: The Electoral Connection.* New Haven: Yale University Press.

Mejova, Yelena, Padmini Srinivasan, and Bob Boynton. 2013. GOP Primary Season on Twitter: 'Popular' Political Sentiment in Social Media. In *Proceedings of the Sixth ACM International Conference on Web Search and Data Mining*, 517–526. Rome.

Molyneux, Logan, Rachel R. Mourão, and Mark Coddington. 2017. US Political Journalists' Use of Twitter: Lessons from 2012 and a Look Ahead. In *Twitter and Elections Around the World: Campaigns in 140 Characters or Less*, ed. Richard Davis, Christina Holtz-Bacha, and Marion R. Just, 43–56. New York: Routledge.

Parmelee, John H., and Shannon L. Bichard. 2012. *Politics and the Twitter Revolution: How Tweets Influence the Relationship Between Political Leaders and the Public.* Plymouth: Lexington Books.

Salem, Sara. 2015. Creating Spaces for Dissent: The Role of Social Media in the 2011 Egyptian Revolution. In *Social Media, Politics and the State: Protests, Revolutions, Riots, Crime and Policing in the Age of Facebook, Twitter and YouTube*, ed. Daniel Trottier and Christian Fuchs, 171–188. New York: Routledge.

Small, Tamara. 2010. Canadian Politics in 140 Characters: Party Politics in the Twitterverse. *Canadian Parliamentary Review* 33 (3): 39–45.

Straus, Jacob R., Matthew E. Glassman, Colleen J. Shogan, and Susan N. Smelcer. 2013. Communicating in 140 Characters or Less: Congressional Adoption of Twitter in the 111th Congress. *PS: Political Science and Politics* 46 (1): 60–66.

Tsugawa, Sho, and Kosuke Kito. 2017. Retweets as a Predictor of Relationships Among Users on Social Media. *PloS One* 12 (1): 1–19.

Tumasjan, Andranik, Timm O. Sprenger, Philipp G. Sandner, and Isabell M. Welpe. 2010. Predicting Elections with Twitter: What 140 Characters Reveal About Political Sentiment. In *Proceedings of the Fourth International AAAI Conference on Weblogs and Social Media*, 178–185. https://www.aaai.org/ocs/index.php/ICWSM/ICWSM10/paper/viewFile/1441/1852

Vargo, Chris J., Lei Guo, Maxwell McCombs, and Daniel L. Shaw. 2014. Network Issue Agendas on Twitter During the 2012 U.S. Presidential Election. *Journal of Communication* 64: 296–316.

Williams, C.B., and G.J. Guliati. 2008. What Is a Social Network Worth? Facebook and Vote Share in the 2008 Presidential Primaries. In *Annual Meeting of the American Political Science Association*, 1–17. Boston.

———. 2012. Social Networks in Political Campaigns: Facebook and the Congressional Elections of 2006 and 2008. *New Media & Society* 15 (1): 52–71.

CHAPTER 4

Candidate Image: When Tweets Trump Tradition

Kim Hixson

Abstract Donald Trump's image as a presidential candidate was unconventional and non-traditional, upturning the long-held beliefs about candidate image and its relationship to electoral success. An analysis of 1687 tweets identifies the attributes of candidate image that are reflected in them. In addition, 157 of his tweets mentioned in newspaper articles were analyzed to provide an indication of the image attributes that gained earned media or "free publicity." Comparing this subset of earned media tweets to all the tweets shows a difference between the candidate-projected image and the media-projected image. One-third of Trump's tweets contained the anger/aggressive attribute, but a much higher percentage of these tweets was mentioned in the newspaper articles. The media coverage of Trump's tweets helped him have a much higher value in earned media than his opponents. This advantage, coupled with his victories, leads to questions about how Trump's tweets will affect candidate messaging and candidate image in future campaigns.

Keywords Twitter • Candidate image • Presidential election • Earned media

K. Hixson (✉)
Utah State University, Logan, UT, USA

© The Author(s) 2018
C.J. Galdieri et al. (eds.), *The Role of Twitter in the 2016 US Election*,
https://doi.org/10.1007/978-3-319-68981-4_4

The election of Donald Trump to the presidency surprised most pundits and befuddled many election analysts. His unconventional style of campaign communication that included personal insults, name-calling ("Crooked Hillary," "Lying Ted Cruz," or "Little Marco,"), and an agenda of intolerance should lead campaign strategists to question long-held beliefs in the importance of a candidate's positive image and character to election victory. Indeed, scholars have long attempted to define the elements and attributes of candidate image. Miller et al. (1985) claimed candidate image is a very important, but little understood, aspect of election politics. In the ensuing years, a single, all-defining description and explanation of image has proved to be elusive, however.

In our classical tradition, we have accepted Aristotle's idea that a speaker must have three qualities—practical wisdom, virtue, and selflessness—present to convince an audience of the speaker's trustworthiness. This concept was applied long ago to the desired character of a candidate in our representative government. A successful campaign for an elected office has many ingredients including money, staff, volunteers, but usually the most salient is the image of the candidate projected to voters. The image of Donald Trump generated by his tweets during the election, along with the massive media coverage of these messages, seems to belie these traditional beliefs of the kind of candidate that voters will support. Trump used belittling remarks and put-downs to disparage others as a focus in his campaign, an act unprecedented in presidential campaigns (Lee and Quealy 2016, p. A10).

The appeal of Trump's candidacy and his tweets led to an increase of more than 300 per cent in the number of Twitter followers during the campaign (Trackalytics.com 2017). Trump tweeted his followers often, and with some of those retweeting his messages, his outreach increased greatly. Furthermore, as this analysis shows, some of his tweets generated free publicity—or earned media—during the campaign providing even wider dissemination of his messages and his image. As Trump's more-provocative tweets were those that garnered most media attention, the prevailing consensus is that Trump's tweets are filled with vitriol and contempt and are malicious in content. Why, then, did the tone and substance of his Twitter persona not alienate his followers and weaken his campaign? What kind of a candidate image was produced and sustained? This analysis seeks to understand how his messaging was effective by revealing the attributes of image Trump communicated in his tweets.

CANDIDATE IMAGE

Scholarly work on candidate image has been somewhat sporadic with most of this research concentrating on US presidential candidates. The media coverage of candidates has played a significant role in the determination of the public's perception of the candidates' images, as this is how most voters encounter candidates. Indeed, voters select a candidate based on the candidate's image or credibility as a source of information (Miller et al. 1985; Trent et al. 1993; Hellweg 2004; Teven 2008). Among the factors identified that form a candidate's image are personal characteristics, integrity, competence, reliability, charisma, honesty, strength, compassion, performance, aggressiveness, and activeness (Miller et al. 1986; Kaid and Chanslor 2004).

Conventional wisdom holds that voters are rational beings. The vote they give to a candidate is earned based on the candidate's beliefs and stands on the issues. Indeed, this idea of the voter weighing the candidates' positive and negative attributes and making a rational, informed decision when voting is rooted in American mythology. Franklin Delano Roosevelt said, "Democracy cannot succeed unless those who express their choice are prepared to do it wisely." Later, Walter Cronkite, CBS Nightly News anchor who was acclaimed to be the "most trusted person in America," took a more cynical view: "We are not educated well enough to perform the necessary act of intelligently selecting our leaders."

Despite Cronkite's viewpoint, in presidential election campaigns, our long-held belief is that the "best" candidate wins the elections. If voters do make a rational choice, then there is no doubt that the "best" candidate will be the winner. Inherent in this idea of "best" is the character of that candidate. To win, it is thought, a candidate must present a positive image that is acceptable. A significant predictor of how people will vote is based on character assessment (Bishin et al. 2006). A generally accepted American belief is that good citizenship requires the intellectual skill of critical thinking and the participatory skills of being aware of what is happening in government. Therefore, a manifestation of good citizenship is the act of making a rational, wise choice when casting a vote.

Research reveals, however, that citizens do not vote based on their rational decision-making, but vote for candidates based more on affective concerns. Voters do assess a candidate's likeability, a quality that is strongly correlated with a candidate's positive image traits of trustworthiness, goodwill, and competence (Teven 2008). Homophily, or the idea that people connect with other people who are similar to them in values and beliefs, drives voter intentions more than any other variable except partisanship (Warner and Banwart 2016). This part of the image of a candidate, the idea that the candidate "cares about people like me," is most salient in building image. The next most influential variable in the makeup of a candidate is a candidate's character. Candidates who articulate the problems of the typical voter are understood to be in touch with the voters and empathetic to their problems. Voters, who believe a candidate does not do so, see the candidate as out of touch or personally aloof (Trent et al. 2001). Apparently, in Trump's tweets he was able to accomplish homophily despite his widely known persona as a billionaire business executive and reality television celebrity persona. As surprising as it seems, many of his voters must have identified with him. This analysis of Trump's tweets shows that he devoted many of his Twitter messages to this necessary articulation.

A candidate's image is a rather vague concept. Kaid (2004) posits that scholars agree that image is a "complex construct." Image is a combination of what a candidate projects and of what a voter perceives. Hacker (2004) puts more emphasis on the voters' contribution to candidate image by explaining it as "clusters of voter perceptions of candidates." Furthermore, a candidate's image as perceived by voters is a strong predictor of candidate choice. Issues, apparently, matter much less. There is, however, a complex interaction between image and issues (Stephen et al. 2004).

Researchers have explored the composition of character in candidates. Kinder (1986) found character based broadly on competence and integrity. Voters use their perception of a candidate's personal character as a heuristic to other aspects of the candidate's image (Sullivan et al. 1990). The impression that a candidate makes on a voter can lead the voter to form an image of the candidate. This image can be based on emotions or feelings (Wu and Coleman 2014) or the impressions of the candidate that a voter believes are important (Hacker and Zahaki 2000). In general, candidate image is the aggregate of persona, the impressions of leadership ability, and the suitability of the candidate for the office in connection with the stand on the issues.

Voters are much more likely swayed to vote by their perception of a candidate's image than by their rational understanding of the candidate's stand on the issues (Wu and Coleman 2014). Simply put, these two researchers noted, "It mattered less what the candidate said than how he said it." Voters have a preconceived notion of an idealized candidate in mind before evaluating a candidate. They compare this ideal candidate to the real candidate. When a strong correlation is found, a voter will be more likely to vote for that candidate (Nimmo 1995).

TWITTER AND SOCIAL MEDIA USE BY CAMPAIGNS

Election campaigns have embraced the use of social media as a fundamental communication channel to voters; however, campaigns do not use it much for an interactive media. Campaigns use social media more as a one-way communication method (Pew, Digital news developments in US presidential campaigns 2000–2016 2016). With careful planning, campaigns can use social media to reach a more dispersed audience than can be attained through television, radio, or newspapers (Metzgar and Marugii 2009).

Social media enables a campaign to give an interpersonal tone to campaign messages. By having the candidate's name appear as the sender of the message, the message to the voter appears to be, and perhaps is, direct from the candidate. A voter might believe that the candidate is personally addressing the voter. This can make social media a highly effective method of campaign communication (Kim et al. 2016). Interpersonal communication has long been recognized as the most effective, although an inefficient, method of encouraging political activism and persuading voters.

This interpersonal characteristic is a great advantage that Twitter provides a candidate. A direct connection to a voter, most likely a supporter, can be accomplished through a cell phone as well as a computer. This connection can have the feel of a genuine interpersonal relationship. The utility of Twitter is enhanced by its qualities as a communication medium. It can distribute a message widely and quickly in an unedited, unfiltered form to an audience nationwide, and Twitter can do so at hardly any cost. It can be extremely useful in reacting to changing political circumstances or serving other needs of a campaign (Kreiss 2016). Twitter use as a political campaign communication medium has increased along with its use by the public as a personal communication medium. Only 11 years old at the time of the general election, Twitter was being used by approximately 67 million Americans (Statista 2016).

THE IMPORTANCE OF EARNED MEDIA IN CAMPAIGNS

Gaining free publicity or "earned media" has long been the goal of political campaigns. In fact, our democracy depends on "earned media" or "free publicity" to provide voters with electoral information and to encourage political discussion (Harris 2016). Campaigns spend a great deal of time and energy on the activity of getting the candidate's name and visage in front of the public as many times and as often as possible. When these mentions in television, radio, newspapers, magazines, and their digital equivalents happen free of charge, precious campaign dollars can be spent elsewhere. Adversely, getting "paid media" is accomplished through the purchasing of media time or space. This "paid media" in campaigns is mostly evident as advertising for the candidate through the traditional media of television, radio, newspapers, magazines, outdoor boards, transit, direct mail, and signage. Additionally, campaigns now have the freedom to transmit messages via "owned media." It might include a website, a blog, or social media accounts such as Facebook, Snapchat, Instagram, and Twitter. All of these platforms are owned and controlled by each campaign.

There are important differences between these three different media types. Most are the costs of the message, the reach of the medium, and the control the campaign has over message content. Earned media provides a very low cost to distribute the message. It has the potential to reach millions of voters, although with little control of selection of the audience. However, earned media provides very little control over the content of the message that is distributed. Paid media has a very high cost in almost all cases. It, too, has the potential to reach millions of voters with somewhat strong control over the selection of the audience. Paid media also provides strong control over the content of the message received by the voters. Owned media has very little cost. It has the potential to reach millions of voters, but most will have to "opt in" or purposely seek out the message. It provides strong control over the audience selection and enables the campaign to have a very high amount of control over the message transmitted.

Given these characteristics for earned, paid, and owned media, it is apparent that using owned media such as Twitter to generate earned media is a strategy that can have great benefits for a campaign. Messages received through earned media are comparable to the traditional notion of "word-of-mouth" advertising: it is believable, as it seems to come from a non-biased source (Stephan and Galak 2012). However, there is a risk in this strategy for a campaign: the possibility that the result will generate "bad publicity" or an unfavorable portrayal of the candidate.

Through the content of his tweets, Donald Trump seemed to be unconcerned with portraying himself in an unfavorable manner. Indeed, this lack of concern has been a Trump habit for some time. According to *The Art of the Deal* (1987), Trump believes that bad publicity can be better than no publicity at all. In the entertainment world, any free publicity, whether good or bad, is referred to as "buzz." For a celebrity, "buzz" is positive. Creating "buzz" and having people talk about the celebrity, usually a movie star, was thought to be good for business.

The traditional view for a political candidate, however, has been to avoid bad publicity. The belief is that bad publicity will cost the candidate votes. The smaller number of news media choices in the past made "bad press" much more difficult for voters to ignore. The damage "bad press" could inflict on a candidate's image was troublesome for a campaign to repair. Campaigns have long tried to avoid this need for "damage control" as tradition holds that "staying on message" by presenting a candidate's planned and focused message is the campaign's aim. Yet, creating "buzz" through social media was the intention of campaigns during the 2012 Republican primaries (Murthy 2015). The campaigns wanted their candidate to be noticed and to be the subject of conversation.

Earned media can be an extension of this "buzz" creation effort as journalists use candidates' tweets to monitor campaigns for information (Parmelee 2014). They receive the same message as the candidate's followers (Fulgoni et al. 2016) increasing the likelihood of "buzz" being launched through earned media. Tweets can provide journalists with easy, quick, and inexpensive access to messages that might provide story ideas or content. Journalists use Tweets for quotes when the candidate is not readily available. For example, during the general election, the *Los Angeles Times* (Finnegan 2016) used three Trump tweets, from 2012, 2013, and 2014, to provide quotes from the candidate mocking global warming.

Earned media results in part from a reciprocal relationship between campaigns and the media (Darr 2016). The media want to provide their viewers and readers with information about the campaigns, and the campaigns need the media to provide as much free publicity as possible. Donald Trump fed both into and off of this relationship by the frequency of his tweets and their interesting content.

METHOD

Content Analysis of Tweets

Tweets were collected from the @RealDonaldTrump Twitter account during the primary elections from 1 January through 7 June and during the general election from 1 September through 8 November 2016. Retweets were not included unless a comment originating from the account was included. Each of 1687 tweets was analyzed for its textual content. Two coders with campaign management experience analyzed each tweet. The coders based their decisions only on the words written. The coders determined, "What attribute of the candidate's image communicated in the tweet is most salient?" In many of the tweets, Trump insinuated that his opponent(s) did not have a particular attribute. The implication is that if an opponent is untrustworthy, then the candidate (Trump) sending the tweet is trustworthy. The attributes of competence/integrity, morality, and confidence/strength were also coded in this manner. The coders tried to solve any disagreement through discussion. Whenever agreement could not be resolved, the tweet was coded as vague or undefinable.

Kaid (2004) notes that scholars generally agree that the complexity in the candidate image construct makes it difficult measure. Many approaches have been used in this quest. Semantic differential scales have become an accepted and oft-used measuring device. In order to determine the attributes of candidate image that might be evident in tweets, we examined the adjectives used in these scales as well as using concepts garnered in the research previously mentioned (Miller et al. 1985, 1986; Trent et al. 1993; Hellweg 2004; Kaid and Chanslor 2004; Teven 2008).

The candidate image attributes evident in the tweets are described below.

Active: contains information about a physical action the candidate has taken, is taking, or will take in the campaign.

Competence/experience: presents a claim that the candidate has the necessary knowledge, capacity, skill, or talent to solve a particular problem.

Trust/integrity: a claim of honesty, reliability, or dependability. The notion of adhering to ethical principles.

Confidence/strength: presents a belief in the power of the candidate to make an event occur or have a successful outcome.

Patriotism: indicates support, defense, or love for the United States or any symbol of the nation. Also may be a show of loyalty to the nation or its symbols.

Morality: a profession of decency and a high regard for virtuous conduct. A profession of the distinction of right and wrong or acting from this distinction.

Fear/paranoia: promoting ideas of evil, terror, danger, or distress; or build suspicion of the motives of those who are, or who might be, in opposition to the candidate or the nation.

Anger/aggression: presents a feeling about a person, subject, belief, or event that is rooted in indignation, outrage, animosity, displeasure. A willingness to make verbal attacks on others or their beliefs.

Friendly: an expression of camaraderie, gratitude, affection, respect, or helpfulness.

Vague/undefined: a tweet that had too little text to be categorized or that did not have a salient attribute.

CONTENT ANALYSIS OF TWEET-RELATED EARNED MEDIA ARTICLES

Newspaper articles were examined to determine the earned media that Trump's tweets generated. An online search was conducted using indexes that searched *The New York Times, The Washington Post, Los Angeles Times, Chicago Tribune, USA Today,* and *The Wall Street Journal.* Newspaper articles selected were those that were published during seven randomly selected weeks during the primary elections and five randomly selected weeks during the general election. The number of times a tweet was mentioned was recorded and matched with its previously determined image attribute.

RESULTS

Candidate Image Attributes Through Tweets

Table 4.1 shows the results of the content analysis of the tweets for the image attribute most salient in each tweet. The frequency of each attribute and its percentage of all tweets are reported. For the primary election, 635 tweets were coded. For the general election, 1052 tweets were coded. Inter-coder agreement was at the high end of the "good" range, Cohen's $\kappa = .801, p < .001$.

A chi-square test for independence was run between the elections and the candidate image attributes. All expected cell frequencies were greater than five. This independence of variables was found to be significant, $\chi^2(9) = 28.468, p < .001$.

Almost one-third (30.6 per cent) of the tweets from the @RealDonaldTrump account were coded as the anger/aggressiveness

Table 4.1 Candidate image attributes by tweets—frequency and percentage

		Frequency		Percentage	
		Primary	General	Primary	General
Active	Count	63	160	9.9	15.2
	Expected count	83.9	139.1		
Competence	Count	55	102	8.7	9.7
	Expected count	59.1	97.9		
Trust/integrity	Count	14	35	2.2	3.3
	Expected count	18.4	30.6		
Confidence/strength	Count	107	173	16.9	16.4
	Expected count	105.4	174.6		
Patriotism	Count	31	42	4.9	4.0
	Expected count	27.5	45.5		
Morality	Count	13	45	2.0	4.3
	Expected count	21.8	36.2		
Fear/paranoia	Count	43	82	6.8	7.8
	Expected count	47.1	77.9		
Anger/aggressiveness	Count	194	268	30.6	25.8
	Expected count	173.9	288.1		
Friendly	Count	91	103	14.3	9.8
	Expected count	73.0	121.0		
Vague/undefined	Count	24	42	3.8	4.0
	Expected count	24.8	41.2		
Total		635	1052	100%	100%

attribute during the primary elections. Closely related conceptually are those tweets that are coded the fear/paranoia attribute (6.8 per cent). Therefore, more than one-third of Trump's tweets was mean-spirited, contemptible, and could arouse an intensity of passion.

The attribute of confidence/strength was found in 16.9 per cent. Friendliness was found in 14.3 per cent. Conceptually related to those two attributes is competence/experience at 8.7 per cent. These three attributes together make up just under 40 per cent of Trump's tweets in the primary. The attribute of activeness was identified in 9.9 per cent of the tweets.

There was a significant, though not huge, difference in the percentage of some attributes in the general election when compared to the primary election. The largest change was in the activeness attribute that increased to account for 15.2 per cent of the general election tweets. Anger/aggressiveness tweets decreased almost five percentage points (25.8 per cent) while those of fear/paranoia increased one percentage point (7.8 per cent). Friendliness decreased to 9.8 per cent while competence increased one percentage point to 9.7 per cent. Confidence/strength decreased, but by only one-half of a percentage point.

Earned Media Generated from Tweets

In the primary election, most of Trump's tweets that received earned media promoted his image of anger/aggression with those promoting his image of fear/paranoia following. Forty-seven articles were found to contain 73 mentions of Trump's Twitter activity with 57 mentions of a specific tweet that was coded in this analysis. The focus of this news coverage was clearly on the tweets that provide an image attribute of anger/aggressive or fear/paranoia with 68 per cent of the tweets presenting one of those image attributes (see Table 4.2).

Several of these anger/aggressive tweets included threats. For example, "Be careful, Lyin' Ted, or I will spill the beans on your wife!" (Trump 2016b, 22 March). An angry tweet sent after Trump's second place finish in the Iowa Caucus reads, "Based on the fraud committed by Senator Ted Cruz during the Iowa caucus, either a new election should take place or Cruz result nullified" (Trump 2016a, 3 February).

In this analysis of the general election, 76 articles had 103 mentions of Trump's Twitter use; 74 of those articles contained 100 mentions of specific tweets. Tweets that promoted the anger/aggression and fear/paranoia image attributes were the most mentioned (see Table 4.3).

Table 4.2 Image attributes of tweets that gained earned media—primary elections

Image attribute	Number of tweets mentioned	Percentage of all tweets mentioned
Anger/aggression	28	49
Fear/paranoia	11	19
Competence	7	12
Confidence/strength	5	9
Four others	6	11
Total	57	100

Table 4.3   Image attributes of tweets that gained earned media—general election

Image attribute	Number of tweets mentioned	Percentage of all tweets mentioned
Anger/aggression	60	60
Fear/paranoia	27	27
Competence	7	7
Active	3	3
Three others	3	3
Total	100	100

Note: This analysis does not include the well-known two-page *New York Times* article documenting Trump's provocative tweets. Those mentions of Trump's tweets would skew the data presented here

DISCUSSION

Through his tweets, Trump promoted an image as an angry, aggressive, paranoid candidate who was active and confident. By inference, his followers recognized his anger and fears mirrored their own. His image of being active and confident, perhaps, led these followers to believe that he could solve the problems that alarmed and troubled them.

The most successful or effective tweets are those that produce earned media as these tweets extended the reach of the message. Tweets coded as "anger/aggressive" and "fear/paranoia" made up 81 per cent of Trump's tweets mentioned in the newspaper stories and further reinforced the image of anger and paranoia. Many of the "anger" tweets getting newspaper coverage were those that dealt with the former Ms. Universe. Although mention of the Ms. Universe situation initially surfaced in the first debate between Clinton and Trump, the Republican nominee added to the "buzz" by his famous early morning tweet, "Did Crooked Hillary help disgusting (check out sex tape and past) Alicia M become a U.S. citizen so she could use her in the debate?" (Trump 2016c, 30 September). This tweet was one of several messages Trump tweeted beginning at 3:00 am. Not only did the content of several of these tweets make news, but also the time he composed and sent the tweets was newsworthy. Mentions of this tweet included news stories as late as 27 October, almost a month after the early morning tweet.

Trump's tweets alleging voter fraud or a rigged election were mentioned in the news stories 16 times making up 10.3 per cent of those mentions. Thirteen of those mentions came during the general election. These tweets provided an image of Trump spreading fear and paranoia as there was never any proof of the allegations. Three weeks before the election, he tweeted,

"The election is absolutely being rigged by the dishonest and distorted media pushing Crooked Hillary – but also at many polling places – SAD" (Trump 2016d, 16 October). A few days later Trump tweeted, "Of course there is large scale voter fraud happening on and before Election Day. Why do Republican leaders deny what is going on? So naive!" (Trump 2016e, 17 October). Ridout and Searles (2011) found that candidates who are trailing in races are more likely to present ads that are negative. The anger/ aggression and fear/paranoia attributes in this study fit in to this idea of negativity. Interestingly, the analysis here shows that Trump had a lower percentage of tweets with these two attributes during the general election than during the primaries. However, the media were more likely to include those types of tweets in their coverage during the general election. Many polls showed that Trump was trailing in the race against Clinton and was on his way to losing the election. Does this explain why the tweets that produced earned media had this negative slant? Did the media believe that these were the most newsworthy because they expected Trump's loss?

Voters are more accepting of angry ads in the last few weeks of a campaign as these negative ads are expected at that time (Ridout and Searles 2011). However, anger appeals in the early stages of a campaign are thought to repel voters. Trump's tweets were negative from the beginning suggesting that scholars' notions were not correct in this election. During the primaries, Trump's anger/aggressive and fear/paranoia tweets made up approximately one-third of his tweets, but these tweets generated two-thirds of the earned media. If Trump's tweets alone provided a significant part of the attributes of his image, the media certainly added weight to this image construction.

Conclusion

Earned media from his tweets was just a part of the huge advantage in free publicity that Trump enjoyed in both the primaries and the general election. Overall, Trump generated earned media valued approximately at $5 billion while Hillary Clinton generated a little more than $3 billion, and through Twitter, he generated twice as much earned media value as his Democratic opponent (Harris 2016). During the primary elections, Trump's earned media advantage over his opponents was even more substantial (Confessore and Yourish 2016). This data from the primaries did not break down the activities that generated the earned media, but it is safe to assume that the value produced through Trump's tweets exceeded the value of his opponents' tweets.

Why were Trump's tweets mentioned many more times than the other candidates' tweets? Why did he receive the gift of much more earned media than did his opponents? Was it that his messaging through tweets was so outrageous, different, and novel?

Many of Trump's tweets were coded as the anger/aggressiveness attribute. Of course, this percentage does not gauge the intensity of the language used. Perhaps it is the intensity or the novelty of the messages when compared to the integrity demonstrated by candidates in past presidential campaigns that led to Trump receiving so much earned media.

With so many of Trump's tweets deemed negative in tone, should we ask, how did he keep his followers on Twitter? Why would they continue to support him? Research has found that candidates who are seen as manipulative usually suffer a loss in credibility (Teven 2008); however, with his followers, it seems Trump did not. A reason for this situation, perhaps, is that 40 per cent of his tweets were of a positive nature.

In the past, voters have placed emphasis on the personal characteristics of honesty and integrity (Trent et al. 2001). So, does the Twitter campaign of Donald Trump signify a transgression of the conventions that have governed presidential election campaign behavior? Have we seen a transformation from a 230-year tradition of integrity and decency in candidate messaging to a no-holds-barred environment where name-calling and lashing out are the norm? Trump has changed the image of what we accept in a presidential candidate as he transgressed the traditional morals we expect. However, there has not been a total transformation in what voters look for in a candidate. Given that homophily is second only to partisanship in driving voter intentions (Warner and Banwart 2016), we can infer that Trump was able to make many voters believe that he shared their values and was looking out for their interests.

Had Trump been defeated in either the primary or the general election, these questions would be far less pertinent. With his victories, however, can we expect to see more of this type of behavior or even more extreme behavior on the part of those who wish to win election to public office? Do we blame the media, in part for this transformation if it has taken place? The media did cover the tweets. Apparently, those tweets that are the most outlandish and unconventional are those that get the earned media that all campaigns covet.

Trump's tweets, and especially those that got media coverage, did not portray his image as that of a traditional candidate. The image portrayed was vastly different from the image we expect a presidential candidate to project, that of a respectful, even-tempered, levelheaded, moral leader of all Americans. However, because those tweets got him so much earned media, it is easy to conclude that the tweets paid off. This unconventional image worked to his advantage. So, has the expectation changed of how a candidate should behave? Along with it, has the candidate image we expect, and will accept, been altered forever? Most certainly, some future candidates will follow Trump and act with little regard for integrity or their character-based image in exchange for the earned media that brashness can attract. Ultimately, voters will decide if our ideals of candidate image have changed, or if the 2016 presidential election was just an aberration.

REFERENCES

Bishin, Benjamin G., Daniel Stevens, and Christian Wilson. 2006. Character Counts? Honesty and Fairness in Election 2000. *Public Opinion Quarterly* 20 (2): 235–248.
Confessore, Nicholas, and Karen Yourish. 2016. The Upshot: $2 Billion Worth of Free Media for Donald Trump. *New York Times*. Retrieved from www.nytimes.com/2016/03/16/upshot/measuring-donald-trumps-mammoth-advantage-in-free-media.html?_r=0
Darr, Joshua P. 2016. Presence to Press: How Campaigns Earn Local Media. *Political Communication* 33 (3): 503–522.
Finnegan, Michael. 2016. Election 2016; Trump Denies Climate Science Amid Rising Seas. *Los Angeles Times*, p. A.1, September 18.
Fulgoni, Gian M., Andrew Lipsman, and Carol Davidsen. 2016. The Power of Political Advertising: Lessons for Practitioners. *Journal of Advertising Research* 56: 239–244.
Hacker, Kenneth L. 2004. Introduction: The Continued Importance of the Candidate Image Construct. In *Presidential Candidate Images*, ed. Kenneth Hacker, 1–19. Lanham: Rowman & Littlefield.
Hacker, Kenneth L., and Walter R. Zakahi. 2000. Components of Candidate Images: Statistical Analysis of the Issue-Persona Dichotomy in the Presidential Candidate of 1996. *Communication Monographs* 67 (3): 227–239.
Harris, Mary. 2016. A Media Post-Mortem of the 2016 Presidential Election. *mediaQuant*, November 16. Retrieved from https://www.mediaquant.net/2016/11/a-media-post-mortem-on-the-2016-presidential-election/

Hellweg, Susan A. 2004. Campaigns and Candidate Images in American Presidential Elections In *Presidential Candidate Images*, ed. Kenneth Hacker, 21–48. Lanham: Rowman & Littlefield.

Kaid, Lynda Lee. 2004. Measuring Candidate Images with Semantic Differentials. In *Presidential Candidate Images*, ed. Kenneth Hacker, 231–236. Lanham: Rowman & Littlefield.

Kaid, Lynda Lee, and Mike Chanslor. 2004. The Effects of Political Advertising on Candidate Images. In *Presidential Candidate Images*, ed. Kenneth Hacker, 133–150. Lanham: Rowman & Littlefield.

Kim, Tonghoon, David J. Atkin, and Carolyn A. Lin. 2016. The Influence of Social Networking Sites on Political Behavior: Modeling Political Involvement Via Online and Offline Activity. *Journal of Broadcasting & Electronic Media* 60 (1): 23–39.

Kinder, Donald. 1986. Presidential Character Revisited. In *Political Cognition*, ed. Richard R. Lau and David O. Sears, 233–255. Hillsdale: L. Erlbaum Associates.

Kreiss, Daniel. 2016. Seizing the Moment: The Presidential Campaigns' use of Twitter during the 2012 Election Cycle. *New Media & Society* 18 (8): 1473–1490.

Lee, Jasmine C., and Kevin Quealy. 2016. All the People, Places and Things Donald Trump Has Insulted on Twitter Since Declaring His Candidacy For The Presidency. *New York Times*, p. A10, October 24.

Metzgar, Emily., and Albert Maruggi. 2009. Social Media and the 2008 U.S. Presidential Election. *Journal of New Communications Research* IV (1): 141–165.

Miller, Arthur H., Martin P. Wattenberg, and Oksana Malanchuk. 1985. Cognitive Representations of Candidate Assessments. In *Political Communication Yearbook 1984*, 183–210. Carbondale: Southern Illinois University Press.

———. 1986. Schematic Assessments of Presidential Candidates. *American Political Science Review* 80: 521–540. https://doi.org/10.2307/1958272

Murthy, Dhiraj. 2015. Twitter and Elections: Are Tweets Predictive, Reactive or a Form of Buzz? *Information, Communication & Society* 18 (7): 816–831.

Nimmo, Dan. 1995. The Formation of Candidate Images During Election Campaigns. In *Candidate Images in Presidential Elections*, ed. Kenneth Hacker, 131–144. Westport: Praeger.

Parmelee, John H. 2014. The Agenda-Building Function of Political Tweets. *New Media & Society* 16 (3): 434–450.

Pew, Digital news developments in U.S. presidential campaigns 2000–2016. 2016. July 18. Retrieved from http://www.journalism.org/2016/07/18/digital-news-developments-in-u-s-presidential-campaigns-2000-2016/

Ridout, Travis N., and Kathleen Searles. 2011. It's My Campaign and I'll Cry if I Want to: How and When Campaigns Use Emotional Appeals. *Political Psychology* 32 (3): 439–458.

Statista.com. 2016. Number of Monthly Active Twitter Users in the United States from 1st Quarter 2010 to 1st Quarter 2017 (in millions). Retrieved from https://www.statista.com/statistics/274564/monthly-active-twitter-users-in-the-united-states/

Stephan, Andrew T., and Jeff Galak. 2012. The Effects of Traditional and Social Earned Media on Sales: A Study of a Microlending Marketplace. *Journal of Marketing Research* XLIX: 624–639.

Stephen, Timothy, Teresa M. Harrison, William Husson, and David Albert. 2004. Interpersonal Communication Styles of Political Candidates: Predicting Winning and Losing Candidates in Three U.S. Presidential Elections. In *Presidential Candidate Images*, ed. Kenneth Hacker, 177–196. Lanham: Rowman & Littlefield.

Sullivan, John L., John H. Aldrich, Eugene Borgida, and Wendy M. Rahn. 1990. Candidate Appraisal and Human Nature: Man and Superman in the 1984 Election. *Political Psychology* 11 (3): 459–484.

Teven, Jason J. 2008. An Examination of Perceived Credibility of the 2008 Presidential Candidates: Relationships with Believability, Likeability, and Deceptiveness. *Human Communication* 11 (4): 391–408.

Trackalytics.com. 2017. The Most Followed Twitter Profiles. Retrieved 6 June, 2017, from http://www.trackalytics.com/twitter/followers/widget/realdonaldtrump/

Trent, Judith S., Paul A. Mongeau, Jimmie D. Trent, Kathleen .E. Kendall, and Ronald B. Cushing. 1993. The Ideal Candidate: A Study of the Desired Attributes of the Public and Media Across Two Presidential Campaigns. *American Behavioral Scientist*, 37(2): 225–239.

Trent, Judith S., Cady Short-Thompson, Paul A. Mongeau, Andrew K. Nusz, and Jimmie D. Trent. 2001. Image, Media Bias, and Voter Characteristics. *American Behavioral Scientist* 44 (12): 2101–2124.

Trump, Donald. 1987. *The Art of the Deal*. New York: Random House.

———. 2016a. [realDonaldTrump]. (2016, 3 February). Based on the Fraud Committed by Senator Ted Cruz During the Iowa Caucus, Either a New Election Should Take Place or Cruz Result Nullified. Retrieved from https://twitter.com/realDonaldTrump/status/694890328273346560

———. 2016b. [realDonaldTrump]. (2016, 22 March). Lyin' Ted Cruz Just Used a Picture of Melania from a G.Q. Shoot in His ad. Be Careful, Lyin' Ted, or I Will Spill the Beans on Your Wife! Retrieved from https://twitter.com/realDonaldTrump/status/712457104515317764?lang=en

———. 2016c. [realDonaldTrump]. (2016, 30 September). Did Crooked Hillary Help Disgusting (Check Out Sex Tape and Past) Alicia M Become a U.S. Citizen So She Could Use Her in the Debate? Retrieved from https://twitter.com/realDonaldTrump/status/781788223055994880

———. 2016d. [realDonaldTrump]. (2016, 16 October). The Election Is Absolutely Being Rigged by the Dishonest and Distorted Media Pushing Crooked

Hillary – But Also at Many Polling Places – SAD. Retrieved from https://twitter.com/realDonaldTrump/status/787699930718695425

———. 2016e. [realDonaldTrump]. (2016, 17 October). Of Course There Is Large Scale Voter Fraud Happening on and Before Election Day. Why Do Republican Leaders Deny What Is Going on? So Naive! Retrieved from https://twitter.com/realDonaldTrump/status/787995025527410688

Warner, Benjamin R., and Mary C. Banwart. 2016. A Multifactor Approach to Candidate Image. *Communication Studies* 67 (3): 259–279.

Wu, H. Dennis, and Renita Coleman. 2014. The Affective Effect on Political Judgement: Comparing the Influences of Candidate Attributes and Issue Congruence. *Journalism and Mass Communication Quarterly* 9 (3): 530–543.

CHAPTER 5

Tweeting on the Campaign Trail: The When, How, and What of Donald Trump's Tweets

Luke Perry and Paul Joyce

Abstract Donald Trump's Twitter activity is among the most controversial elements of his political rise. Reactions by journalists and politicians have been overwhelmingly negative, yet Trump has undeniably revolutionized the use of Twitter in presidential elections and the presidency. This chapter examines Trump's use of Twitter by analyzing every one of Trump's tweets for when, what, and how Trump tweeted as a candidate and president elect. Negative and emphatic tweets were most prevalent and most popular. Trump's "successful" Twitter approach raises many questions about his presidency and the future of presidential campaigns. This is just the beginning of what is poised to become a rapidly growing area of scholarly focus in campaigns and elections.

Keywords Twitter usage • Negative attacks • Campaign • Election

Donald Trump's Twitter activity is among the most controversial elements of his political rise. Reactions by journalists and politicians have been

L. Perry (✉) • P. Joyce
Utica College, Utica, NY, USA

© The Author(s) 2018
C.J. Galdieri et al. (eds.), *The Role of Twitter in the 2016 US Election*,
https://doi.org/10.1007/978-3-319-68981-4_5

overwhelmingly negative, generating disinterest (Savransky 2017), offense (Forbes 2017), skepticism (Bump 2016), ridicule (Johnson and Phillip 2017), and deep concern (Walsh 2017). Responses by political scientists have lamented the lost possibilities of e-democracy (Samuel 2017), urged Trump to stop tweeting for the good of his presidency, and the presidency as an institution (Musgrave 2017), and even debated whether Twitter should remove Trump for violating its rules regarding harassment (Masket 2017; Azari 2017). Trump has undeniably revolutionized the use of Twitter in presidential elections and the presidency. This chapter examines Trump's use of Twitter by coding and analyzing every one of Trump's tweets between securing the nomination and being inaugurated.

TWITTER AND ELECTORAL POLITICS

As Towner and Dulio suggest, "The Internet has provided a wealth of opportunities for candidates and their campaigns to use technology in creative and innovative ways" (2012, 95). Social networking sites, in particular, have been utilized by a substantial segment of the voting age population for over a decade and reflect the "next Internet generation, which is primarily user driven" (Gueorguieva 2008, 288). The medium is low cost, and it helps lesser known candidates get name recognition, share their message, recruit volunteers, and raise money. For years digital media was identified "as a channel with the potential to increase the focus on the personal side of politics" (Karlsen and Enjolras 2016, 339). Social media has enabled candidates to increasingly connect with electorates independent of party (Balmas et al. 2014; Karlsen 2011; Zittel 2009), transforming the media landscape into a "hybrid media system" whereby campaigns target different audiences through various forms of media (Chadwick 2013). Twitter is now used by candidates and their followers to influence and drive news cycles in a direction that is most favorable to them.

Social media's impact on agenda setting is a major focus of political communication scholarship. Groshek and Groshek suggest that "agenda setting is no longer conceived of as a top-down process from mainstream print and broadcast media to audiences," but also a dynamic process where citizens reporting in online spaces "can give shape and definition to media and policy agenda among the public" (2013, 16–17). Social media is also valuable for scholars seeking to understand public opinion. Twitter "records people's immediate reaction in real time but without the unnatural settings of focus groups" (Cornell Chronicle 2016). These viewpoints are time-stamped, so they can be compared over an extended period. Political communication scholars have demonstrated greater appreciation for the impact of social media than the population at large. This may be beginning to change. Drew Margolin concluded that 2016 "will be the campaign where we learn that Twitter matters in the way that television mattered for the Nixon-Kennedy debates" (Cornell Chronicle 2016).

Scholarship of Twitter and electoral politics has focused on content and engagement. Scholars have found that members of Congress primarily use Twitter as "vehicles of self-promotion" to post information, particularly "links to news articles, blog posts, and ...[their] daily activities" (Golbeck et al. 2010, 1612). Their tweets tend "not to provide new insights into government or the legislative process or to improve transparency," but Twitter can "facilitat[e] direct communication between Congress people and citizens" (Golbeck et al. 2010, 1612). Similar findings are evident in other Western democracies. In the United Kingdom, legislators predominately used Twitter during election time "as a unidirectional form of communication," though there are some candidates who interacted with voters, by mobilizing, helping, and consulting with them (Graham et al. 2013, 73). In Australia politicians have attempted "to use Twitter for political engagement, though some are more successful in this than others" (Grant et al. 2010, 579). Those seeking to converse, rather than broadcast, appeared to gain greater political benefit.

Barack Obama first brought Twitter to the US presidency in a meaningful way and became more effective with the platform over time. Twitter was not developed enough to play a significant role in the 2008 presidential campaign. Obama adopted a more transparent profile during his 2012 reelection campaign, generating greater volume of tweets and more original tweets (Adams and McCorkindale 2013). Other candidates in the campaign retweeted sparingly but did not reply, missing a valuable opportunity to create meaningful dialogue with potential supporters. In line with previous findings, candidates as a whole were more interested in disseminating information than engaging in two-way conversation. Barack Obama had the highest level of engagement as the only candidate to ask questions of followers and retweet these questions, demonstrating they were read.

Twitter and presidential elections broke new ground during the 2016 campaign. The debates were the most tweeted in history (White 2016). Live tweeting became a normalized part of political analysis for news organizations and bloggers, including political scientists; however, negative political sentiment on Twitter was high (Cornell Chronicle 2016). This illuminates how Twitter reflects and feeds America's deep polarization. Supporters on both sides of the campaign spent a lot of time criticizing each other over social media. So did their respective robot armies. More than one third of pro-Trump tweets and nearly one fifth of pro-Clinton tweets between the first and second debate were from automated accounts, exceeding one million total (Guilbeault and Wooley 2016).

EMPIRICAL ANALYSIS OF TRUMP'S TWEETING

I think that maybe I wouldn't be here if it weren't for Twitter
—Trump's statement in a post-election interview
on Fox News. (Schwartz 2017)

Scrutiny of Trump's tweeting intensified during the transition and the first six months of his presidency. This produced countless anecdotal and stereotypical accounts of his Twitter behavior, illuminating a need for greater comprehensive and empirical analysis. We examined every one of Trump's tweets between informally securing the nomination on May 25, 2016, through Inauguration Day, January 20, 2017. There were 1229 tweets from @realDonaldTrump over 241 days. Our analysis focused on four questions:

1. When did Donald Trump tweet?
2. How did Trump tweet?
3. What did Trump tweet about?
4. What tweets were most circulated?

Six different time blocks were used to measure when Trump tweeted. Most of Trump's tweeted occurred in the morning, between 5:01 am and 9:00 am, which accounted for 26 percent of his total tweets. Trump also tweeted consistently during the afternoon, 22 percent of his tweets occurred between 1:01 pm and 5:00 pm, and early evening, another 22 percent of his tweets occurred between 5:01 pm and 9:00 pm. Trump tweeted less frequently later in the evening, just 3 percent of his tweets occurred between 9:01 pm and 1:00 am, and overnight. Ten percent of Trump's tweets occurred between 1:01 am and 5:00 am. This is significant, given the

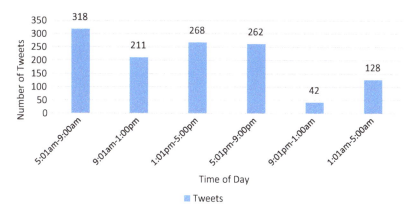

Fig. 5.1 Times of day that Trump tweeted

infrequency of previous political communication during these hours, but does not support the notion that Trump tweeted frequently overnight.

Sean Spicer, White House Press Secretary, shared in January that Trump's tweets were not coordinated or shared in advance with him. Trump "drives the train on this," explained Spicer, who woke up and read the tweets because it "drives the news" (Janssen 2017). Many journalists and new organizations have followed suit. The traditional news cycle no longer exists, thanks in part to Trump's tweeting (Uberti 2017, Fig. 5.1).

Three categories were developed to examine how Trump tweeted, through statement, question, or exclamation. Trump used exclamation points in 59 percent of his tweets. This was more common than statements, which constituted 36 percent of his tweets. Trump clearly did not use the medium as a forum to raise questions. Only 61 of his tweets were questions, just 5 percent of the total, and nearly all of the questions raised were rhetorical. A substantial portion of Trump's tweets (262 tweets, 21 percent of the total) used all caps, the digital equivalent of yelling. This was measured through binary analysis (did or did not) on top of examining whether Trump's tweets were exclamations, statements, or questions. All caps was clearly a sustained part of Trump's Twitter style as he employed this linguistic device in one of every five tweets (Fig. 5.2).

Four categories were created to measure what Trump tweeted about: (1) going negative, (2) info sharing, (3) giving thanks, and (4) encouragement. Trump went negative early and often. Negative attacks constituted

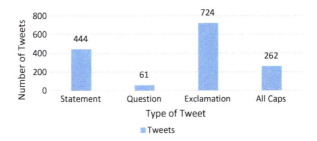

Fig. 5.2   How Trump tweets

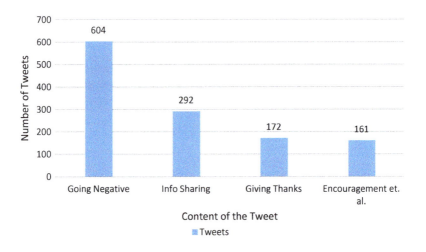

Fig. 5.3   What Trump tweets

nearly half his tweets. Trump shared information in just 24 percent of his tweets, historically the most typical use of social media by candidates. Trump gave thanks in 14 percent of his tweets, primarily to those who endorsed him and audiences he spoke before. He provided encouragement and/or sought to make sense of an event or tragedy in 13 percent of his tweets. None of Trump's tweets included replies to other Twitter accounts. Trump occasionally quoted a tweet but that was the extent of the interaction. Trump's reliance on one-way communication contrasts previous studies of successful Twitter use by candidates, which suggested two-way communication is most effective (Fig. 5.3).

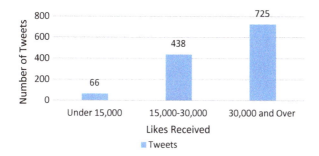

Fig. 5.4 Range of "Likes" received by Trump

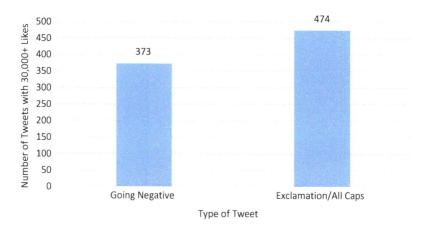

Fig. 5.5 Emotion and high-frequency tweets

Three thresholds were developed to measure how liked Trump's tweets were. Most of Trump's tweets received 30,000 likes or more. Of those most liked tweets, over half of them were negative and 65 percent of them included an exclamation point or all caps. This suggests that Trump's most popular tweets were the ones that were more negative and emphatic (Figs. 5.4 and 5.5).

Four categories were developed to measure how liked Trump's tweets were. Seventy percent of Trump's tweets were retweeted 9000 times or more. Within this group of most retweeted tweets, over half of them were negative and 64 percent of them included an exclamation point or all caps.

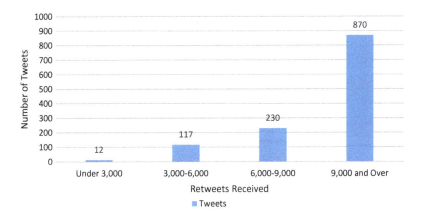

Fig. 5.6 Range of retweets received by Trump

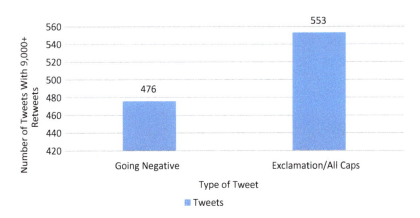

Fig. 5.7 Emotion and high-frequency retweets

This was remarkably consistent with our findings regarding likes and similarly suggests that the most retweeted tweets were the ones that were more negative and emphatic (Figs. 5.6 and 5.7).

CONCLUSIONS

Three main conclusions can be drawn from this analysis. First, while Donald Trump generated attention for occasional late night tweets, he actually did not tweet frequently late at night or during the very early morning hours. Tweets after 9:00 pm and before 5:00 am were only 13 percent of his total tweets. Second, Donald Trump went negative more frequently and communicated more loudly on Twitter than any previously successful presidential candidate. Presidential candidates on Twitter is a relatively recent, but growing, phenomena. Finally, doing so was well received by his supporters as measured both in likes and retweets. Using all caps was particularly well received. This was present in nearly two-thirds of Trump's likes and retweets. Going negative is common in other forms of campaign communication, such as television commercials, so this was not completely foreign. At the same time, having these negative tweets come directly from the candidate's Twitter account, 24 hours a day, was a new development.

Looking ahead, there are key questions regarding Trump and Twitter. First, will Donald Trump maintain or modify his tweeting behavior as president? Early analysis suggests that Trump's first 100 Days exhibited a decline in going negative and an increase in information sharing (Perry and Joyce 2017). At the same time, Trump's tweeting during this period was otherwise consistent in regard to our other measurements, including his use of exclamation points and all caps. This suggests that the substance changed some, but not the style.

Further questions are broader and more speculative. What can future presidential campaigns learn from Trump's use of Twitter in 2016? Should two-way communication still be the goal of campaigns in light of Trump's success forgoing this? How can future candidates duplicate the passion and emphatic approach that benefitted Trump while also reducing the abrasiveness that simultaneously turned off large portions of the electorate?

It is hard to envision a future presidential candidate being as devoted and personal in her/his Twitter usage. That said, any challenger to President Trump, in a general campaign, or a primary, will have to develop a comprehensive strategy for how to employ social media, if for no other reason, than to play defense against Trump. This strategy, in part, will likely seek to replicate Trump's populism and raw ability to connect with supporters, while dispensing with some or much of the vitriol. Whether a candidate can have one without the other will be tested during this era of strong political polarization.

Donald Trump contributed to the shattering of several conventional norms. For better and worse, Trump has revolutionized Twitter in presidential campaigns and politics. This is just the beginning of what is poised to become a rapidly growing area of scholarly focus in campaigns and elections.

REFERENCES

Adams, Ameilia, and Tina McCorkindale. 2013. Dialogue and Transparency; A Content Analysis of How the 2012 Presidential Candidates Used Twitter. *Public Relations Review* 39 (4): 359.

Azari, Julia. 2017. Trump Should Keep Tweeting. *Vox.* https://www.vox.com/mischiefs-of-faction/2017/6/30/15900538/trump-tweeting-transparency. Accessed 18 Aug 2017.

Balmas, Meital, Gideon Rahat, Tamir Sheafer, and Shaul R. Shenhav. 2014. Two Routes to Personalized Politics: Centralized and Decentralized Personalization. *Party Politics* 20 (1): 37–51.

Bump, Philip. 2016. Now You Can Fact-Check Trump's Tweets- in the Tweets Themselves. *The Washington Post.* https://www.washingtonpost.com/news/the-fix/wp/2016/12/16/now-you-can-fact-check-trumps-tweets-in-the-tweets-themselves/?utm_term=.84f3f44d5301. Accessed 18 Aug 2017.

Chadwick, Andrew. 2013. *The Hybrid Media System.* New York: Oxford University Press.

Cornell Chronicle. 2016. Interview with Drew Margolin, Professor of Communication at Cornell University. http://news.cornell.edu/stories/2016/10/qa-how-twitter-key-presidential-campaigns-2016. Accessed 18 Aug 2017.

Forbes. 2017. Donald Trump's 10 Most Offensive Tweets. https://www.forbes.com/pictures/flji45elmm/donald-trumps-10-most-of/#10da6dd070df

Golbeck, Jennifer, Justin Grimes, and Anthony Rodgers. 2010. Twitter Use by the U.S. Congress. *Journal of the American Society for Information Science and Technology,* 61. http://hcil2.cs.umd.edu/trs/2009-32/2009-32.pdf. Accessed 18 Aug 2017.

Graham, Todd, Marcel Broersma, Karin Hazelhoof, and Guido van't Haar. 2013. Between Broadcasting Political Messages and Interacting with Voters. *Information, Communication and Society,* 16(5). http://www.tandfonline.com/doi/abs/10.1080/1369118X.2013.785581. Accessed 18 Aug 2017.

Grant, Will, Brenda Moon, and Janie Busby Grant. 2010. Digital Dialogue? Australian Politician's Use of the Social Network Too Twitter. *Australian Journal of Political Science,* 45(4). http://www.tandfonline.com/doi/abs/10.1080/10361146.2010.517176. Accessed 18 Aug 2017.

Groshek, Jacob, and Megan Clough Groshek. 2013. Agenda Trending: Reciprocity and the Predictive Capacity of Social Networking Sites in Intermedia Agenda Setting Across Topics Over Time. *Media and Communication* 1 (1): 16–17.

Gueorguieva, Vassia. 2008. Voters, My Space, and You Tube; The Impact of Alternative Communication Channels on the 2006 Election Cycle and Beyond. *Social Science Computer Review* 26 (3): 288.

Guilbeault, Douglas, and Samuel Woolley. 2016. How Twitter Bots Are Shaping the Election. *The Atlantic.* https://www.theatlantic.com/technology/archive/2016/11/election-bots/506072/. Accessed 18 Aug 2017.

Janssen, Kim. 2017. Trump's Spokesman Has No Idea What He'll Tweet Next. *The Chicago Tribune.* http://www.chicagotribune.com/news/chicagoinc/ct-trump-aide-uc-chicago-inc-20170104-story.html. Accessed 18 Aug 2017.

Johnson, Jenna, and Abby Phillip. 2017. "It's Really Not Normal": Both Sides Condemn Trump for Vulgar Tweet About TV Host. *The Washington Post.* https://www.washingtonpost.com/politics/it-is-really-not-normal-both-sides-condemn-trump-for-vulgar-tweet-about-tv-host/2017/06/29/ce1030e4-5ce4-11e7-9b7d-14576dc0f39d_story.html?utm_term=.f84f1b4a06dd. Accessed 18 Aug 2017.

Karlsen, Rune. 2011. A Platform for Individualized Campaigning? Social Media and Parliamentary Candidates in the Party-Centered Norwegian Campaign. *Policy & Internet* 3 (4): 1–25.

Karlsen, Rune, and Bernard Enjolras. 2016. Styles of Social Media Campaigning and Influence in a Hybrid Political Communication System. *International Journal of Press/Politics* 21 (3): 339.

Masket, Seth. 2017. Trump Won't Drop Twitter, But Twitter Should Drop Trump. *Pacific Standard.* https://psmag.com/news/trump-wont-drop-twitter-but-twitter-should-drop-trump. Accessed 18 Aug 2017.

Musgrave, Paul. 2017. President Trump Should Stop Tweeting. Now. *The Washington Post.* https://www.washingtonpost.com/posteverything/wp/2017/06/08/president-trump-should-stop-tweeting-now/?utm_term=.a15d356a01f3. Accessed 18 Aug 2017.

Perry, Luke, and Paul Joyce 2017. In 3 Charts Here's How President Trump's Tweets Differ from Candidate Trump's Tweets. *The Monkey Cage.* https://www.washingtonpost.com/news/monkey-cage/wp/2017/05/02/in-3-charts-heres-how-president-trumps-tweets-differ-from-candidate-trumps-tweets/?utm_term=.f7da92baafd9. Accessed 18 Aug 2017.

Samuel, Alexandra. 2017. How Trump's Twitter Presidency Hijacked Hopes for E-Democracy. *JSTOR Daily.* https://daily.jstor.org/how-trumps-twitter-presidency-hijacked-hopes-for-e-democracy/. Accessed 18 Aug 2017.

Savransky, Rebecca. 2017. London Mayor on Trump Tweets: 'I Really Don't Care.' *The Hill.* http://thehill.com/business-a-lobbying/336533-london-mayor-on-trump-tweets-i-really-dont-care. Accessed 18 Aug 2017.

Schwartz, Ian. 2017. Trump: "I Wouldn't Be Here if It Wasn't for Twitter". *Real Clear Politics.* https://www.realclearpolitics.com/video/2017/03/15/trum p_i_wouldnt_be_here_if_it_wasnt_for_twitter_i_have_my_own_form_of_media. html. Accessed 18 Aug 2017.

Towner, Terri, and David Dulio. 2012. News Media and Political Marketing in the United States: 2012 and Beyond. *Journal of Political Marketing* 11: 95–119.

Uberti, David. 2017. Trump Killed the News Cycle. *Columbia Journalism Review.* https://www.cjr.org/criticism/donald-trump-news-cycle-slow-news-day.php. Accessed 18 Aug 2017.

Walsh, Ken. 2017. A Dangerous Game. *U.S. News and World Report.* https:// www.usnews.com/news/the-report/articles/2017-06-09/president-trumps-dangerous-twitter-game. Accessed 9 June 2017.

White, Daniel. 2016. This Was the Most Tweeted Presidential Debate ever. *Time.* http://time.com/4508981/presidential-debate-twitter-clinton-trump/. Accessed 18 Aug 2017.

Zittel, Thomas. 2009. Lost in Technology? Political Parties and Online Campaigns of Constituency Candidates in Germany's Mixed Member Electoral System. *Journal of Information Technology & Politics* 6: 298–311.

CHAPTER 6

Donald Trump, Naturally: Revisionist Environmental Policy, Global Warming Tweets, and the Unexpected Emphasis on Climate Change in the 2016 Campaign

Mark J. O'Gorman

Abstract Does Donald Trump's social media record explain his evolving environmental policy? How has Mr. Trump's novel political communication strategy, his tens of thousands of Twitter posts ("tweets"), evolved in frequency, form, and content during his political transformation from pre-candidate gadfly to presidential candidate and then as the 45th US President? No policy in the early months of President Trump's Republican administration had greater transformation than environmental policy, from vivid advocacy of fossil fuel and coal energy production, broad ecological regulatory evisceration, and the US decoupling from the Paris Climate Accord. Given that Donald Trump, less than a decade ago, advocated greater global climate change (gcc) action, Twitter analysis of the ecological contrasts and contradictions between citizen Trump and the 45th US President provides insights on how his 2009–2016 climate change, energy,

M.J. O'Gorman (✉)
Maryville College, Maryville, TN, USA

© The Author(s) 2018
C.J. Galdieri et al. (eds.), *The Role of Twitter in the 2016 US Election*,
https://doi.org/10.1007/978-3-319-68981-4_6

and environmental tweets explain part of his unique political, and planetary, worldview.

Keywords   Twitter • Global warming • Climate change • Communication strategy

> We should be focusing on beautiful, clean air & not on wasteful & very expensive GLOBAL WARMING bullshit! China & others are hurting our air.[1]
>
> —Donald J. Trump, Twitter Post, December 15, 2013c, 5:07:49 AM, *@realDonaldTrump*

> The concept of global warming was created by and for the Chinese in order to make U.S. manufacturing non-competitive.
>
> —Donald J. Trump, Twitter Post, November 6, 2012, 2:15:52 PM, *@realDonaldTrump*

Donald J. Trump achieved a measure of ecological, political, and personal triumph with his June 1, 2017, announcement from the White House Rose Garden, stating that the United States was ceasing "all implementation" of the United Nations (UN) Paris global climate change (gcc) agreement (Trump "Statement...Climate Accord" 2017c). Building on populist rhetoric that he was "elected to represent the citizens of Pittsburgh, not Paris," President Trump's decoupling announcement affirmed his 2016 campaign promises (Cohn 2017). It also affirmed a unique set of economic and environmental arguments, embracing Mr. Trump's vision of a "hobbled America, ransacked by pointless environmental regulation," to validate his climate accord withdrawal decision (Milman 2017a, b; Trump "Statement...Climate Accord" 2017c).

Some of President Trump's history with climate change policy is famous for its contrast and contradictions. So disgusted with gcc policy during Barack Obama's administration that he famously stated in early 2014 that "[t]his very expensive GLOBAL WARMING bullshit has got to stop" (Donald J. Trump, Twitter Post, January 1, 2014b, @realDonaldTrump). Yet, in December 2009, NY businessman Donald Trump endorsed and co-sponsored a full-page ad in the *New York Times* asking then-President Obama and the US Congress to work harder "to ensure meaningful and effective measures to control climate change" (Adler and Leber 2016; Sheehan and Harrington 2017). How can his evolution of thinking on these issues be analyzed? What can be revealed from the 2016 campaign that may help unpack the 45th President's worldview on climate change?

One theme, after analyzing Mr. Trump's gcc journey, is that he deserves credit for keeping gcc an active part of the 2016 US presidential campaign narrative. Presidential candidates since the 1980 campaign have shared their concerns about climate change (Bailey 2015, 52–57). But, as with past electoral disappointments among environmentalists, neither environmental nor climate change issues ranked among those most impacting voters on Election Day 2016 ("2016 Campaign...Top Voting Issues" 2016). Even Barack Obama's environmental security threat rhetoric during the 2012 campaign, equating gcc with other national security or existential threats, barely moved the salience needle among voters (O'Gorman, in Holder and Josephson 2014). Although a climate denier and dismissive of the topic, his social media record provides interesting insights on how he connects economics and energy to gcc. Specifically, review of his tweets (Trump Twitter Archive 2017).

Donald Trump's past and more current climate-related Twitter include the surprise that Trump *very rarely* tweeted about climate change during his campaign run. His many climate tweets almost all occurred pre-campaign, prior to his June 2015 presidential campaign announcement. His older gcc tweets became fodder for his opponents, including GOP opponents and Democrats Bernie Sanders and Hillary Clinton, including a tangential mention of gcc by Clinton in the second presidential debate in October 2016 (Lavelle 2016).

In a still embryonic information transition from television to social media, review of his environmental tweets does provide lessons on what elements comprise the 45th President's vision of the planet. Review of Trump's climate Twitter architecture may reveal hints at a conscious strategy by the Trump campaign, an approach which combined tweets and outsized campaign trail rhetoric in order to lift Donald Trump to the White House. If so, this strategy may be worth exploring, to help political observers understand what communication about climate change, or any issue, may yet emanate from the Trump White House.

THE MAD GENIUS OF DONALD TRUMP'S TWITTER
COMMUNICATION STRATEGY

Policies and issues are useless for election purposes. . . .The shaping of a candidate's integral image has taken the place of discussing conflicting points of view.

—Marshall McLuhan, in Joe McGinniss, *The Selling of the President, 1968,* 1969

Not since Franklin D. Roosevelt's radio "fireside chats" and John F. Kennedy's televised press conference performance have US presidential media use been so scrutinized as have been the Twitter posts, "tweets" of Donald J. Trump. Regardless of one's opinion of the medium, the political fallout of his over 31,000 tweets posted since he began in May 2009 is inescapable ("Here's Donald. . .," 2017).[2] The author glowingly describes his own tweets as "MODERN DAY PRESIDENTIAL," which helped him win 2016 Presidency in one of the greatest upsets in US political history (Donald J. Trump, Twitter Post, July 1, 2017a, @realDonaldTrump).

Republican strategists and Trump supporters applaud his tweet use as a way to circumvent traditional media reportage. They extol Trump's self-described "honest and unfiltered message," as an authentic means to activate his base by giving his "fans what they want" (Donald J. Trump, Twitter Post, June 6, 2017b, @realDonaldTrump, and Chmielewski 2016.). Such tweeting also permits Mr. Trump to drive home his policy message and vision, insuring "in an age where there is a wealth of information, [but] always a poverty of attention," President Trump can control the story line via massive media coverage each time he generates a tweet (Walsh 2017).

Trump's Twitter strategy reinforces, and creatively amends, Jakob Nielsen's participation inequality rule as to social media/online communities, where 90% with social media account observe or lurk, 9% contribute occasionally, and only the final 1% provide the most content (Nielsen 2006). Trump's continual tweeting, combined with follower/contributors who repost and reaffirm his tweets, magnify Trump's social media presence. While Trump's Twitter account attracted 20 million followers in January 2017, that number was less than half of those following Barack Obama on social media, and far behind entertainment personalities with follower numbers approaching 100 million ("Donald Trump Reaches Landmark. . ." 2017).

The Trump campaign's recognition to have Trump become a Nielsen "heavy contributor," as soon as possible, in order to provide a mechanism for the other 99% of "intermittent contributors" and "lurkers" to respond to such tweet activity (Nielsen 2006). Regardless of those revering or reviling by Mr. Trump's tweets, or skeptical that he is the sole author of all of his tweets, his social media use allows him a platform mostly unfettered by print/television media, permitting this part of his campaign to be distinct, which helped him gain support and gather momentum to break from the crowded Republican presidential nomination field in late 2015.

Such a social media strategy in politics comes at a price and creates a Faustian bargain, maintaining continual interest among an ever-changing global social media audience, while broadening one's online appeal. In the hyper-competitive world of social media ratings, overcoming non-representation is paramount. As Nielsen wrote in 2006, if a US political party "nominates a candidate supported by the 'netroots,' it will almost certainly lose because such candidates' positions will be too extreme to appeal to mainstream voters." Because political blog postings come from less than 0.1% of voters, or the same 1% of users (Nielsen 2006), the political fear is that social media popularity equates with narrow electoral support. The social media brand must entertain to attract and maintain interest but also be broadly appealing to gather in wide demographic support.

Trump is the exception. Intense far-right and alternative-right (alt-right) supporters passionately supported him online as his focus on "a toxic civic culture" is inciting race and immigration fears (Morgan 2017; Green 2017). Trump's non-social media message on the campaign trail further tapped into the "anxiety, nostalgia and mistrust" themes among millions of disaffected Americans that swept him to victory (Jones et al. 2015). Interest in Trump translated into unexpected aid for him on the campaign trail, with him garnering $4.6 billion in free television media coverage during the 2016 race (Saba 2016).

Critics of Trump's Twitter strategy focus on the diminishing support his Twitter use has created and the linguistic limits of this communication method as a policy communication (Binckes 2017). By far, the greatest criticism rests upon Mr. Trump himself: on how his continuous tweets diminish respect for the office he holds and disable attempts by his administration to govern, and growing disgust for the inappropriate and caustic use of this social media format as the 45th President's official communication outlet.

Polling and social media activity in the early days of Trump's administration revealed decreased interest, with 62% of Trump tweets receiving "likes" in the first 50 days of his administration and only 10% of his tweets getting to such levels in the second 50 days of his administration (Glassman and Diamond 2017). June 2017 polling shows 69% of voters think President Trump uses Twitter too much, including 53% among Republicans (Levy 2017).

Trump's caustic Twitter language is now near legend and provides a political Rorschach test for the American electorate. Supporters revel in how, as one TN supporter gushed, Trump's tweets show that he

[is] yet to [be] tame[d]...by the inside-the-Beltway establishment...He's showing us how to win again, how to take back our country...He's going in the face of all these dissenting voices about his tweeting, facing them head on and saying, 'Excuse me, we're not going to do what you say anymore.' This is what got us down the path of losing our country, letting the deep state and left-wing media take over. (Miller and Dinan 2017)

Trump and his campaign better connected to the deep dissatisfaction in America, especially among conservative middle- and working-class voters. While hardly erudite, his capacity to capture this anger via 140-character social media tweets found immediate resonance among disaffected Americans. Sadly, Ott argues that Twitter favors the "politics of debasement" by its capacity to elevate "simple, impulsive and uncivil" dialogue (Ott 2017). Trump's gcc tweets seem to provide a clear case study that demonstrates such language and behavior.

TRUMP'S CLIMATE TWEETING: FREQUENCY, FORM, AND CONTENT

Donald J. Trump's Twitter use follows four distinct eras. One timeframe is from May 4, 2009, until June 15, 2015, the time of his first tweet until the day before he announced his presidential candidacy. The second era is his time as US presidential candidate, from June 16, 2015, until Election Day November 8, 2016. The third era is from the day after the election until his inauguration, November 9, 2016, till January 20, 2017. The final stage involves tweeting during his days as US President, from January 21, 2017, to present.

Frequency: Gadfly Obsession but Not as Candidate

Content analysis of climate-related tweets found on the trumptwitterarchive .com website reveals that official candidate Trump rarely tweeted about climate change, even less so as President. Trump has not sent a tweet with the phrase global warming (g.w.) nor climate change (c.c.), in the first 160+ days as President. Nor did he tweet about this subject as President-elect. Of the 106 Trump g.w. tweets between 2009 and his inauguration day on January 20, 2017, 105 were sent during his pre-candidacy time (prior to June 15, 2015, Trump's presidential candidacy announcement day). He sent *only one* global warming tweet during his time as a presidential candidate. Trump sent 38 tweets containing the phrase climate change, with *only one* sent after he announced his presidential run. The other 37 c.c. tweets were sent during his "gadfly" era outside of politics, when he was a television personality, eponymous real estate developer, and private citizen policy critic on social media. He sent one global warming and one climate change tweet in that same time. Twenty-four of Trump's tweets sent during his gadfly era had both phrases (c.c. and g.w.) in the same tweet. Neither of his two campaign-era g.w./c.c. tweets combined both phrases. The word hoax, a signature phrase used by climate change deniers to explain the falsity of gcc science, was used by Trump 14 times up to the point he became President-elect (17 times up to June 2017 and 12 during his gadfly era). But only eight of the hoax tweets were related to global warming and all occurred prior to his campaign. Recent hoax-worded tweets by President Trump focus on his denying media reports of Trump campaign connections to Russian hacking of the 2016 US election (Manchester 2017).

In contrast, other topics central to Mr. Trump's campaign were frequently tweeted during his campaign, and even more frequently during his pre-candidacy, gadfly era. Mr. Trump's time as candidate, from June 15, 2015, to November 8, 2016, has tweets containing the phrases coal, energy, or jobs were much more frequent (4, 39, and 42 tweets, respectively), again, while only one global warming and one climate change tweets being sent in that same time. But during his gadfly/pre-candidate era, the tweets on these topics grew greatly. Mr. Trump sent out 29 coal-worded tweets, 104 energy-worded tweets, and 306 tweets with the phrase jobs in them.

Trump's ascendancy to the White House has connections to the volume and tone of his pre-candidacy gadfly era tweeting. Trump's tweets jumped significantly from his 56 tweets in 2009. Tweeting 142 times in 2010 and

774 times in 2011, Trump began his shift in tone that provided him cachet with far-right social media followers (Green 2017). After frequent threats over 20 years that he would run for political office, including the US Presidency, a series of 2011 public opinion polls affirmed Mr. Trump was a solid contender among the far-right and/or Tea Party wings of the Republican Party (Blumenthal 2011). His tweets before and after those polls were particularly caustic toward the Obama administration, including the first tweets by Trump questioning Obama's citizenship and birth heritage (Cheney 2016). And the increase in his tweet frequency suggests he found his voice as a public advocate of birther advocates and other alternative-right (alt-right) critics of Obama and extremist critics of a so-called bloated US government.

Form: Trump's T^3 Climate Twitter Architecture—Topic, Target/Threat, Trump-Being-Trump

Trump's pre-candidacy tweets provide the most content about his gcc thinking. They also reveal a consistent attack style of Twitter writing that Trump used frequently in the run up to the 2016 election. It will be called the T^3 style—Topic, Target/Threat, Trump-Being-Trump.

Twitter's 140-character limit compels the tweeter to focus on action words, "communicating a sense of urgency," and to balance between creating a unique social media voice and the tone appropriate to the situation (Seiter 2014). To some, Trump's climate tweets follow a pattern of Aristotelian logos, ethos, and pathos (Hess 2016). But with a level of loathing unique to the 45th President. The T^3 pattern of Trump's tweets starts by identifying the topic to be addressed. Then, in mid-tweet, language focuses on the target (group, person, or issue) to loath and/or the threat that needs to be addressed. Finally, a brief emotional reaction by the author, done in a uniquely Trumpian way—letting "Trump Be Trump"—the phrase that is a personal homage to his off-the-cuff, unencumbered-with-facts and combative style that has been his hallmark (or Achilles heel, depending upon your view of him) in this campaign cycle (Zurcher 2017).

An April 3, 2013b, Trump tweet reveals the entire T^3 pattern. Trump wrote: "Another freezing day in the Spring – what is going on with 'global warming'? Good move changing the name to 'climate change' – sad!" (Twitter Post, @realDonaldTrump) The first third of the tweet identified the topic of an unseasonably cold day. Trump then immediately makes the connection to the target/threat revealed by the topic, skeptical wonder as to whether global warming is real. Finally, an emotive ending "– sad!" that permitted Mr. Trump to provide an opinion on the topic.

Content analysis of the trumptwitterarchive.com website reveals that between 2009 and 2015, Donald Trump sent out 144 tweets related to global warming or climate change. Trump sent 106 tweets with the phrase global warming, and 38 tweets with the phrase climate change. A subset of 24 Trump tweets contained both phrases. Every tweet in the two separate categories was negative, with Trump's critical or dismissal of climate change's validity. All 24 tweets with both phrases combined were negative in tone. Specifically, in the 24 tweets with both phrases, many of the tweets had an emotive Trump-Being-Trump criticism usually found at the end (the final ten words) of his most critical T^3 tweets. Ten phrases in this gcc tweet subset were non-contextual exclamatory final phrases (in italics below) like *"sad!,"* *"lost!,"* *"nonsense,"* *"doesn't work/didn't work"* (at the end of two tweets), or *"wasn't working"* (five tweets) (Matthews 2017 and trumptwitte rarchive.com). Most phrases required reading the entire tweet to understand Trump's sarcastic final criticism of some aspect of gcc policy, as shown in tweet endings like *"Come on people, get smart!" "(aka global warming),"* or to understand weather references, Trump's tweet use to contradict gcc *"too cold!"* (the ending in two tweets) (Matthews 2017 and trumptwittera rchive.com).

Trump used the phrase hoax in 17 of his tweets, with eight of 17 focused on climate change. His gcc hoax phrases are December 6, 2013, till February 5, 2014, to describe gcc in early 2014, with two tweets describing *"global warming hoaxsters"* (Trump Twitter Posts January 29, 2014c, and February 5, 2014a, trumptwitterarchive.com, and Matthews 2017), presumably climatologists and mainstream media who, in concert, are falsely fomenting gcc belief. Mr. Trump provides anecdotal weather evidence in the remaining six climate hoax tweets, as a means to dismiss climate change. And T^3 tweet architecture occurs as well. Temperature forms the introductory topic of five gcc tweets, with phrases *"Ice caps at record size," "Tremendous cold wave," "Massive record setting snowstorm and freezing temperatures"* (two tweets), and *"Another freezing day"* (Matthews 2017 and trumptwitterarchive.com). Mr. Trump's inaccurately connects short-term weather patterns as examples of long-term climate change. Magnifying gcc misunderstandings (NASA—"What's the Difference...," 2005). The hoaxsters listed above formed the target/threat middle part of two tweets. Hoax forms the Trump-Being-Trump (TBT) closing phrase in four of his eight tweets. A dollar sign (\$) forms the final TBT phrase in two of Trump's gcc tweets (Matthews 2017 and trumptwitterarchive.com).

Mr. Trump's dollar sign closing begins to provide economic evidence of his climate change worldview, tweeted prior to his campaign and then affirmed on the 2016 campaign trail. Unconventional and yet not unsurprising, Mr. Trump's climate tweet content was consistent, in its own way.

Content: Conventional Climate Change Thinking and Trump's gcc Revisionism

American economic disaster, based upon inaccurate and false climate science, which duped and led past US governments to create horribly inaccurate regulatory and manufacturing policy, framed Mr. Trump's climate schema in the months prior to his presidential run. While consistent in delivering this message, numerous flaws rested in the climate-thinking content he brought forth on social media.

Trump tweeted on November 6, 2012: "The concept of global warming was created by and for the Chinese in order to make U.S. manufacturing non-competitive" (Donald J. Trump, Twitter Post, @realDonaldTrump). As Chinese Vice Foreign Minister Liu Zhenmin stated in November 2016, climate change negotiations were "initiated by the IPCC [Intergovernmental Panel on Climate Change] with the support of the Republicans during the Reagan and senior Bush administration during the late 1980s" (Shankelman 2016). The late 2014 US-China Climate Change Agreement, where leaders of both nations—the world's two largest polluting nations—agreed to reduce carbon dioxide (CO_2) pollution and to assert leadership for the 190 other countries who were working to ratify the Paris Climate Accord (Biello 2014).

Given Mr. Trump's inability to accept that anthropogenic climate change has occurred for the past 150 years, with evidence confirming such impacts accepted by over 90% of the world scientific community, Mr. Trump's denial tweets are not surprising. But Donald J. Trump's interpretation of climatological data is incorrect. The US Global Change Research Program reports that US average temperature has increased 1.3–1.9F since 1895, with the increase occurring mainly since 1970 (Melillo et al. 2014, p. 20), with 16 of the past 17 warming years on record occurring on Earth since 2001 (NASA "NOAA Data Shaw 2016 Warmest..." 2017). The strong relationship between increased greenhouse gas (GHG) emissions by human activities, including CO_2, and increased temperatures (anthropogenic global warming, or AGW) is accepted as the consensus reason for global warming by 97% of the scientific community (Cook et al. 2013).

Two groups of Trump's tweets do target weaknesses in the gcc community's ability to describe the urgency of the gcc problem. Eleven of Mr. Trump's c.c. tweets criticize the change in focus from global warming to climate change. Trump jumps on the new nomenclature, suggesting it is a disingenuous name change. On June 14, 2014, Trump tweeted: "They only changed the term to CLIMATE CHANGE when the words GLOBAL WARMING didn't work anymore. Come on people, get smart!" (Donald J. Trump, Twitter Post, @realDonaldTrump). Other tweets describe "so-called climate change" (September 17, 2014) or place climate change in quotes (May 7, 2014, and June 8, 2014) as another means of dismissing the phrase (TrumpTwitterArchive, @realDonaldTrump).

Confusion over the use of the more scientifically accurate phrase climate change to discuss this phenomenon, which incorporates a larger range of AGW impacts (e.g. rising sea levels, longer droughts, ocean temperature rise), has led to problems among laypersons and politicians attempting to describe risks related to this issue (Werndl 2016). A recent survey confirmed that 90% of Americans surveyed do not know about the 97% consensus on AGW among the scientific community (Leiserowitz et al. 2017, 4). Trump sows this confusion with his suspicious AGW tweets. However, 70% of respondents in the same survey believe global warming is happening, with over 60% believing AGW is important to them (ibid).

A second group of Trump tweets targets a long-term prioritization critique among environmentalists that gcc is less important to address as are immediate pollution crises from fouled water or food security and provides a lower return on investment, as Bjorn Lomborg has suggested (Lomborg 2001, 2010). Trump on October 11, 2015, tweeted: "President Obama was terrible on @60Minutes tonight. He said CLIMATE CHANGE is the most important thing, not all of the current disasters!" (Donald J. Trump, Twitter Post, @realDonaldTrump). On December 15, 2013, he tweeted: "We should be focusing on beautiful, clean air & not on wasteful & very expensive GLOBAL WARMING bullshit! China & others are hurting our air" (Donald J. Trump, Twitter Post, @realDonaldTrump). The latter was one of three famous "bullshit" climate tweets, when Mr. Trump vented his frustration with wasteful climate policy by the Obama administration.

President Trump's Environmental Protection Agency (EPA) Administrator Scott Pruitt's statement during Trump's Paris Accord withdrawal ceremony applies Lomborg's argument further, but inaccurately. Pruitt said further US climate was not needed, because "America had reduced its $CO2$ footprint to levels from the early 1990s. In fact, between the years 2000 and 2014, the United States reduced its carbon emissions by 18-plus percent" (Trump "Statement...Climate Accord" 2017c). While CO_2 reductions have occurred, as one of the world's largest CO_2 emitters, US carbon emission volume still exacerbates climate change, a concern driving the Obama-Xi climate deal and the Paris Treaty.

US manufacturing job loss outweighs—Trump's, if you will—all other issues for Trump, and was a centerpiece of his climate criticism. Whether caused by poorly negotiated free trade agreements, "onerous" environmental regulations, unnecessary climate treaties like the Paris Accord, Trump believes such actions "could cost America as much as 2.7 million lost jobs by 2025...including 440,000 manufacturing jobs" (Holden et al. 2017, and Trump "Statement...Climate Accord" 2017c). Conservatives validating Trump's concerns are opposed by other scholars who identify systemic changes in technology and robotics that reduce the need for human assemblers, shift toward other areas in advanced manufacturing requiring updated worker training and skill sets and supply chain efficiencies, have fostered much of the three-decade decline of US manufacturing jobs (Muro 2016).

Trump spoke on the campaign trail, happily championing coal and fossil fuel energy development, eager to endorse the Obama-halted Keystone XL pipeline, as long as it was built with "American steel and fabricate[d] in America" (Rosza 2017). He mockingly spoke about having to use pump hair spray rather than aerosol (and GHG emitting) spray because "it's bad for the ozone," even though his NYC apartment was "sealed" and would not harm the atmosphere (Federal News Service 2016). Trump's tweets echoed such themes, championing the US coal industry or railing against President Obama's environmental regulations: "Obama's coal regulations will destroy the coal industry, put Americans out of work, raise electricity prices & lead to blackouts" (Donald J. Trump, Twitter Post, September 23, 2013a, @realDonaldTrump). Of the 36 Trump tweets with the phrase coal, many railed against Obama's coal regulations, with phrases "war on coal" or "assault on coal"(four tweets), "destroy the coal industry" (once), "stupidly closing all its coal plants" (once), and "zero credibility" (once) (TrumpTwitterArchive, @realDonaldTrump).

Trump suggests we are selling all our coal to China. As he tweeted on October 17, 2012: "The US is stupidly closing all of its coal fired plants while at the same time we're selling our coal to China--and then we wonder why our energy costs are going up" (Donald J. Trump, Twitter Post,

@realDonaldTrump, and TwitLonger 2012). The American Geosciences Institute (AGI) and the US Energy Information Administration confirm that the largest US coal export markets are the Netherlands, South Korea, and India, with exporters to all Asian counties averaging just 25% of all US coal exports (US EIA 2013; AGI 2017).

Manufacturing scholars disagree with Mr. Trump's choice of which manufacturing jobs to save. The US Department of Energy (US DOE) reports that 187,117 worked in coal, natural gas, and oil power plants compared to 374,000 people in the solar industry (Korosec 2017). The US coal industry, according the Bureau of Labor Statistics (BLS), employs just over 50,000 workers, with fewer coal workers than workers at Disney World (Thompson 2017). Trump, embracing conservative and far-right economic isolationist thought, and with a clear eye on the US Electoral College map, targeted upper-Midwest and rural Northeastern states and those workers who lost such jobs: "Great meeting w/ coal miners & leaders from the Virginia coal industry- thank you! #MAGA" (Donald J. Trump, Twitter Post, August 10, 2016, @realDonaldTrump). Those hit hardest by manufacturing reductions, believing they were unfairly targeted through overreaching environmental regulations and the renewable energy folly that was fostered by inaccurate climate change, formed the basis of Trump's electoral base. His tweets first stated such beliefs, however uncertain their factual base. Factually fragile, but impossible to ignore, the attention given to his tweets insured some part of his unique climate narrative would resonate with some part of the American electorate.

PRESIDENT TRUMP AND CLIMATE CHANGE: TRUMP DELIVERS ON HIS TWEETS

However stark a contrast between early and then pre-presidential candidate Trump, his excoriation of gcc as a hoax burdening America with too many regulations, thereby killing US jobs, did not stop with his inauguration. The revisionist climate thinking of President Trump's continued in the first few months of his administration, with massive proposed funding cuts in the FY2018 budget for the US Environmental Protection Agency (EPA), the US Department of the Interior, and other environmental science and climate change research and Trump's selection of pollution deregulation champion Scott Pruitt as EPA administrator (Meyer 2017). Among other environmental policy changes are:

- Approving the Dakota Access and Keystone XL pipelines
- Removal of a rule preventing coal mining companies from dumping mining debris (overburden) into local streams
- Overturning a hunting ban on predators in Alaskan wildlife refuges
- Withdrawing federal agency inclusion of GHG emissions in environmental reviews
- Ordering review and potential elimination of rules protecting tributaries and wetlands as part of the US Clean Water Act
- Removal of climate change language from multiple US agency webpages
- Ordering a reevaluation of the Obama administration power plant GHG reduction initiative, the Clean Power Plan. (Popovish and Scholossberg 2017; Greshko et al. 2017)

The irony is that the economic-cum-fossil-fuel nationalism of President Trump misses opportunities to embrace the twenty-first-century US manufacturing that resolves many of the economic concerns of his electoral base. While Mr. Trump sees what global energy Consultant McKinsey and Company see, that is, "the majority of the planet's electricity needs will still be fueled by coal and natural gas in 2040," he chooses to ignore that "nonhydro renewables could more than triple their share of the global power supply by 2040," with much of the growth coming from wind and solar deployment (Nyquist 2016; Nyquist and Maryika 2016). As with the current administration, energy development on the planet, over the next few decades, will be a world of "contradiction and continuity" as fossil fuels remain dominant, while renewable energy growth continues to accelerate (Nyquist and Maryika 2016).

World Resources Institute lists the top US states for wind, solar, and energy efficiency jobs. Michigan and Iowa were ranked sixth and seventh for wind jobs; Ohio ranked tenth for solar jobs, and Michigan and Ohio ranked fifth and ninth for energy efficiency jobs (Jaeger 2017), with these states, and Pennsylvania hosting industries connected to the wind power supply chain (Ayee 2009). All of the states just listed were states that were victorious for Obama in 2008 and 2012 and then "flipped" to Donald Trump in 2016, helping to secure his Electoral College upset. Jobs at wind farms and/or wind-manufacturing facilities are located in 70% of US congressional districts, with the top ten US congressional districts producing the most wind energy in districts all represented by Republicans (Nebsit 2017). The irony is that Mr. Trump may be ignoring one of the fastest growing manufacturing industries in America because of his biased and tweet-laden misbelief that renewable energy is a bad investment (Samuelson 2017). Mr. Trump will be, if anything, unpredictable with his social media use. But his climate tweets during the buildup to his campaign contained flawed policy that is being implemented during the early days of President Trump's administration. As to the topic of climate change and how it impacted his policy platform, he was consistent. Mr. Trump's desire to reject gcc, and to dismantle the US climate change and environmental administrative state, continues. Such policies, beloved by some, while reviled by others, will certainly create a reaction. There is little doubt that, if so moved, he will be nothing but candid with his next tweet describing his views about the planet and America's role in caring for it. An ever more climate turbulent planet waits and wonders.

NOTES

1. All Twitter comments in this chapter are verbatim, including imprecise capitalization, punctuation, and grammar.
2. Counts vary as to Trump's Twitter count, ranging from a low of 31,222 (trumptwitterarchive.com) to a high of 35,973 (trumptweetcounter.com). TrumpTwitterArchive speaks of 4000 tweets deleted by Trump prior to September 2016.

REFERENCES

2016 Campaign: Strong Interest, Widespread Dissatisfaction: 4. Top Voting Issues in 2016 Election. 2016. *Pew Research Center.* July 7. http://www.people-press.org/2016/07/07/4-top-voting-issues-in-2016-election/. Accessed 23 June 2017.
Adler, Ben, and Rebecca Leber. 2016. Donald Trump Once Backed Urgent Climate Action. Wait, What? *Grist.* June 8. http://grist.org/politics/donald-trump-climate-action-new-york-times/. Accessed 21 June 2017.
American Geosciences Institute. 2017. How Much Coal Does the U.S. Export and Import? https://www.americangeosciences.org/critical-issues/faq/how-much-coal-does-us-export-and-import. Accessed 7 July 2017.
Ayee, Gloria. 2009. Marcy Lowe and Gary Gereffi. Manufacturing Climate Solutions: Chapter 11: Wind Power. Center on Globalization Governance and Competitiveness, CGGC/Duke. http://www.cggc.duke.edu/environment/climatesolutions/greeneconomy_Ch11_WindPower.pdf. Accessed 6 July 2017.

Bailey, Christopher J. 2015. *US Climate Change Policy*. Ashgate. https://books. google.com/books/about/US_Climate_Change_Policy.html?id=ZdwyCwAA QBAJ. Accessed 23 June 2017.

Biello, David. 2014. About the U.S.-China Climate Change Agreement. *Scientific American*. November 12. https://www.scientificamerican.com/article/eve rything-you-need-to-know-about-the-u-s-china-climate-change-agreement/. Accessed 6 July 2017.

Binckes, Jeremy. 2017. Think About It: There's a Solution to President Trump's Twitter Problem. *Salon*. June 8. http://www.salon.com/2017/06/08/think-about-it-theres-a-solution-to-president-trumps-twitter-problem/. Accessed 23 June 2017.

Blumenthal, Mark. 2011. Trump's Polls: A Reality Check. *Huffington Post*. June 12. http://www.huffingtonpost.com/2011/04/12/trumps-polls-reality-check_n _848043.html. Accessed 5 July 2017.

Cheney, Kyle. 2016. No, Clinton Didn't Start the Birther Thing. This Guy Did. *Politico*. September 16. http://www.politico.com/story/2016/09/birther-mo vement-founder-trump-clinton-228304. Accessed 5 July 2017.

Chmielewski, Dawn. 2016. Meet Donald Trump's Twitter Whisperer. *Recode*. January 27. https://www.recode.net/2016/1/27/11589146/meet-donald-trumps-twitter-whisperer. Accessed 23 June 2017.

Cohn, Alicia. 2017. Pittsburgh, Not Paris' Rally at White House Thanks Trump. *The Hill*. June 3. http://thehill.com/homenews/administration/336219-group-ga thers-at-white-house-for-pittsburgh-not-paris-rally-thanking. Accessed 21 June 2017.

Cook, John, Dana Nuccitelli, Sarah A. Green, Mark Richardson, Bärbel Winkler, Rob Painting, Robert Way, Peter Jacobs, and Andrew Skuce. 2013. Quantifying the Consensus on Anthropogenic Global Warming in the Scientific Literature. *Environmental Research Letters* 8(2). IOP Publishing Ltd., http://iopscience.io p.org/article/10.1088/1748-9326/8/2/024024/meta#artAbst

Donald Trump Reaches Landmark 20 Million Followers on Twitter – But Is Still Far Behind Barack Obama. 2017. *London (UK) Telegraph*. January 17. http:// www.telegraph.co.uk/technology/2017/01/17/donald-trump-reaches-landma rk-20-million-followers-twitter/. Accessed 5 July 2017.

Federal News Service. 2016. Transcript of Donald Trump's Dec. 30 Speech in Hilton Head, S.C. January 20. http://www.kansascity.com/news/local/news-columns-blogs/the-buzz/article55604115.html. Accessed 6 July 2017.

Glassman, Mark, and Jeremy Scott Diamond. 2017. People Are Liking Trump's Tweets Less. *Bloomberg*. May 5. https://www.bloomberg.com/graphics/2017-trump-twitter-popularity/. Accessed 27 June 2017.

Green, Joshua. 2017. The Remaking of Donald Trump. *Bloomberg*. July 6. https:// www.bloomberg.com/news/features/2017-07-06/the-remaking-of-donald-trump. Accessed 6 July 2017.

Greshko, Michael, Laura Parker, and Brian Clark Howard. 2017. A Running List of How Trump Is Changing The Environment. *National Geographic*, June 14. http://news.nationalgeographic.com/2017/03/how-trump-is-changing-science-environment/. Accessed 6 July 2017.

Here's Donald Trump's First Tweet. 2017. *Fox News*. May 4. http://www.foxnews.com/tech/2017/05/04/heres-donald-trumps-first-tweet-ever.html. Accessed 2 July 2017.

Hess, Amanda. 2016. How Trump Wins Twitter. *Slate*. February 18. http://www.slate.com/articles/technology/future_tense/2016/02/donald_trump_is_the_best_at_twitter_here_s_why.html. Accessed 23 June 2017.

Holden, Emily, Dylan Brown, Benjamin Storrow, and Scott Waldman. 2017. Factcheck Shows Trump's Climate Speech Was Full of Misleading Statements. *Scientific American*. June 2. https://www.scientificamerican.com/article/factcheck-shows-trumps-climate-speech-was-full-of-misleading-statements/. Accessed 76 July 2017.

Jaeger, Joel. 2017. What Are the Top 10 States for Clean Energy Jobs? *World Resources Institute*. April 6. http://www.wri.org/blog/2017/04/what-are-top-10-states-clean-energy-jobs. Accessed 6 July 2017.

Jones, Robert P., Daniel Cox, Betsy Cooper, and Rachel Lienesch. 2015. Anxiety, Nostalgia, and Mistrust: Findings from the 2015 American Values Survey. *PRRI*. http://www.prri.org/research/survey-anxiety-nostalgia-and-mistrust-findings-from-the-2015-american-values-survey/

Korosec, Kirsten. 2017. U.S. Solar Jobs Jumped Almost 25% In the Past Year. *Fortune*. February 7. http://fortune.com/2017/02/07/us-solar-jobs-2016/. Accessed 6 July 2017.

Lavelle, Marianne. 2016. Climate Change Treated as Afterthought in Second Presidential Debate. *InsideClimateNews*. October 10. https://insideclimatenews.org/news/10102016/presidential-debate-town-hall-donald-trump-hillary-clinton-climate-change-global-warming. Accessed 6 July 2017.

Leiserowitz, A., E. Maibach, C. Roser-Renouf, S. Rosenthal, and M. Cutler. 2017. *Climate change in the American mind: May 2017*. New Haven/Fairfax: Yale Program on Climate Change Communication, Yale University/George Mason University.

Levy, Gabrielle. 2017. Poll: President Trump's Tweets Hurt Presidency, Country. *U.S. News & World Report*. June 7. https://www.aol.com/article/news/2017/06/07/poll-president-trumps-tweets-hurt-presidency-country/22130849/. Accessed 27 June 2017.

Lomborg, Bjorn. 2001. *The Skeptical Environmentalist: Measuring the Real State of the World*. Cambridge: Cambridge University Press.

———. 2010. *Cool It: The Skeptical Environmentalist's Guide to Global Warming*. New York: Vintage.

Manchester, Julia. 2017. Trump: Russian Hacking 'A Big Dem HOAX. *The Hill.* June 22. http://thehill.com/homenews/news/338938-trump-russian-hacking-claims-a-big-dem-hoax. Accessed 5 July 2017.

Matthews, Dylan. 2017. Donald Trump Has Tweeted Climate Change Skepticism 115 Times. Here's All of It. *Vox.* June 1. https://www.vox.com/policy-and-poli tics/2017/6/1/15726472/trump-tweets-global-warming-paris-climate-agreement. Accessed 20 June 2017.

McGinniss, Joe. 1969. *The Selling of the President, 1968.* New York: Trident Press.

Melillo, Jerry M., Terese (T.C.) Richmond, and Gary Y. Yohe, eds. 2014. *Highlights of Climate Change Impacts on the United States: The Third National Climate Assessment.* Washington, DC: U.S. Global Change Research Program.

Meyer, Robinson. 2017. What Does Trump's Budget Mean for the Environment? *The Atlantic.* May 24. https://www.theatlantic.com/science/archive/2017/05/trump-epa-budget-noaa-climate-change/527814/. Accessed 23 June 2017.

Miller, S.A., and Stephen Dinan. 2017. Trump's Supporters Urge Him to Keep Tweeting and Taking on the Establishment. *Washington Times.* June 6. http://www.washingtontimes.com/news/2017/jun/6/donald-trumps-twitter-feed-wel come-change-to-suppo/. Accessed 1 July 2017.

Milman, Oliver. 2017a. An Annotated Version of Trump's Climate Speech. *Slate.* June 2. http://www.slate.com/articles/health_and_science/climate_desk /2017/06/donald_trump_doesn_t_understand_climate_change_or_economic s.html. Accessed 21 June 2017.

———. 2017b. Fact Check: Trump's Paris Climate Claims Analyzed. *The Guard-ian.* June 1. https://www.theguardian.com/environment/ng-interactive /2017/jun/02/presidents-paris-climate-speech-annotated-trumps-claims-anal ysed. Accessed 21 June 2017.

Morgan, Jonathon. 2017. How the 'Alt-Right' Came to Dominate the Comments on Trump's Facebook Page. *The Atlantic.* January 21. https://www.theatlantic. com/politics/archive/2017/01/how-the-alt-right-influenced-trump-supporte rs-language-on-facebook/513593/. Accessed 6 July 2017.

Muro, Mark. 2016. Manufacturing Jobs Aren't Coming Back. *MIT Technology Review.* November 18. https://www.technologyreview.com/s/602869/man ufacturing-jobs-arent-coming-back/. Accessed 6 July 2017.

National Aeronautics and Space Administration. 2005. NASA – What's the Differ-ence Between Weather and Climate? *NASA.* February 1. https://www.nasa.go v/mission_pages/noaa-n/climate/climate_weather.html. Accessed 6 July 2017.

———. 2017. NASA, NOAA Data Show 2016 Warmest Year on Record Globally. *NASA.* January 18. https://www.nasa.gov/press-release/nasa-noaa-data-sho w-2016-warmest-year-on-record-globally. Accessed 6 July 2017.

Nebsit, Jeff. 2017. Clean Energy Is Seeing Monumental Job Growth. *U.S. News and World Report.* March 15. https://www.usnews.com/news/at-the-edge/article s/2017-03-15/clean-energy-is-seeing-explosive-job-growth-dont-let-budget-kill-it. Accessed 6 July 2017.

Nielsen, Jakob. 2006. The 90-9-1 Rule for Participation Inequality in Social Media and Online Communities. *NN/g Neilsen Norman Group*. October 9. https://www.nngroup.com/articles/participation-inequality/. Accessed 27 June 2017.

Nyquist, Scott. 2016. Energy 2050: Insights from the ground Up. *McKinsey*. November. http://www.mckinsey.com/industries/oil-and-gas/our-insights/energy-2050-insights-from-the-ground-up. Accessed 6 July 2017.

Nyquist, Scott, and James Maryika. 2016. Renewable Energy: Evolution Not Revolution, March. https://www.mckinsey.com/industries/oil-and-gas/our-insights/renewable-energy-evolution-not-revolution. Accessed 5 Oct 2017.

O'Gorman, Mark. 2014. Natural Uncertainty: Reconciling the Contrasting Environmental Goals of America's First Natural Security President – Barack Obama – Chapter 13. In *The American Election 2012*, ed. R. Ward Holder and Peter B. Josephson. New York: Palgrave Macmillan.

Ott, Brian J. 2017. The Age of Twitter: Donald J. Trump and the Politics of Debasement. *Critical Studies in Media Communication* 34(1): 59–68. http://www.tandfonline.com/doi/full/10.1080/15295036.2016.1266686. Accessed 1 July 2017.

Popovish, Nadja, and Tatiana Scholossberg. 2017. 23 Environmental Rules Rolled Back in Trump's First 100 Days. *New York Times*. May 2. https://www.nytimes.com/interactive/2017/05/02/climate/environmental-rules-reversed-trump-100-days.html?mcubz=0. Accessed 6 July 2017.

Rosza, Matthew. 2017. Trump Delivers Campaign Speech in Iowa After a Local Newspaper Asked Him to Stop Holding Rallies. *Salon*. June 22. http://www.salon.com/2017/06/22/trump-delivers-campaign-speech-in-iowa-after-a-local-newspaper-asked-him-stop-rallies/. Accessed 6 July 2017.

Saba, Jennifer. 2016. Breakingviews: Trump's $4.6 Billion in Free Media. *CNBC*. September 30. http://www.cnbc.com/2016/09/30/breakingviews-trump-cold-shoulder-for-tv-ads-may-set-the-trend.html. Accessed 6 July 2017.

Samuelson, Kate. 2017. Renewable Energy is Creating Jobs 12 Times Faster Than the Rest of the Economy. *Fortune*. January 27. http://fortune.com/2017/01/27/solar-wind-renewable-jobs/. Accessed 6 July 2017.

Seiter, Courtney. 2014. A Scientific Guide to Writing Great Tweets: How to Get More Clicks, Retweets and Reach. *Buffer Social*. May, 6. https://blog.bufferapp.com/writing-great-tweets-scientific-guide. Accessed 1 July 2017.

Shankelman, Jess. 2016. China Tells Trump That Climate Change Is No Hoax It Invented. *Bloomberg*. November 16. https://www.bloomberg.com/news/articles/2016-11-16/china-tells-trump-that-climate-change-is-no-hoax-it-invented. Accessed 6 July 2017.

Sheehan Perkins, Madeleine, and Rebecca Harrington. 2017. It's 'An Expensive Hoax' – And Other Things Trump Has Said About Climate Change. *Business Insider*. June 3. http://www.businessinsider.com/donald-trump-climate-change-global-warming-beliefs-2017-6. Accessed 6 July 2017.

Thompson, Derek. 2017. The White House Exaggerated the Growth of Coal Jobs by About 5,000 Percent. *The Atlantic.* June 6. https://www.theatlantic.com/business/archive/2017/06/pruitt-epa-coal-jobs-exaggerate/529311/. Accessed 6 July 2017.

Trump, Donald J. 2012. *Twitter Post,* November 6, 2:15:52 p.m., https://twitter.com/realDonaldTrump

———. 2013a. *Twitter Post,* September 23, 3:49:33 p.m., https://twitter.com/realDonaldTrump

———. 2013b. *Twitter Post,* April 3, 4:14:13 a.m., https://twitter.com/realDonaldTrump

———. 2013c. *Twitter Post,* December 15, 5:07:49 a.m., https://twitter.com/realDonaldTrump

———. 2014a. *Twitter Post,* February 5, 5:57:14 a.m. https://twitter.com/realDonaldTrump

———. 2014b. *Twitter Post,* January 1, 7:07:56 a.m., https://twitter.com/realDonaldTrump

———. 2014c. *Twitter Post,* January 29, 1:36:45 a.m., https://twitter.com/realDonaldTrump

———. 2015. *Twitter Post,* October 11, 8:43:08 p.m., https://twitter.com/realDonaldTrump

———. 2016. *Twitter Post,* August 10, 3:37:58 p.m., https://twitter.com/realDonaldTrump

———. 2017a. *Twitter Post,* July 1, 05:41:58 p.m., https://twitter.com/realDonaldTrump

———. 2017b. The FAKE MSM Is Working So Hard Trying to Get Me Not to Use Social Media. They Hate that I Can Get the Honest and Unfiltered Message Out. @realDonaldTrump. 7:58 AM, June 6.

———. 2017c. Statement by President Trump on the Paris Climate Accord. *The White House.* June 1. https://www.whitehouse.gov/the-press-office/2017/06/01/statement-president-trump-paris-climate-accord. Accessed 19 June 2017.

Trump Twitter Archive. 2017. http://www.trumptwitterarchive.com/. Accessed 15 Mar 2017.

TwitLonger. 2012. *Twitter Post,* @realDonaldTrump. March 12. http://www.twitlonger.com/show/gd1eek. Accessed 7 July 2017.

U.S. Energy Information Administration. 2013. 25% of U.S. Coal Exports Go to Asia, but Remain a Small Part of Asia's Total Coal Imports. *Today in Energy.* June 21. https://www.eia.gov/todayinenergy/detail.php?id=11791

Walsh, Kenneth T. 2017. Trump Uses Twitter as Strategic Weapon. *U.S. News and World Report.* January 6. https://www.usnews.com/news/ken-walshs-washington/articles/2017-01-06/trump-uses-twitter-as-strategic-weapon. Accessed 27 June 2017.

Werndl, Charlotte. 2016. On Defining Climate and Climate Change. *British Journal for the Philosophy of Science* 67(2): 337–364. https://academic.oup.com/bjps/article/67/2/337/2473104/On-Defining-Climate-and-Climate-Change. Accessed 6 July 2017.

Zurcher, Anthony. 2017. Trump: Unchained and Unapologetic. *BBC News.* February 16. http://www.bbc.com/news/world-us-canada-38996292. Accessed 5 July 2017.

CHAPTER 7

Can We at Least All Laugh Together Now? Twitter and Online Political Humor During the 2016 Election

Todd L. Belt

Abstract This chapter evaluates the differences in humorous content found on Twitter versus other social media sites during the 2016 presidential election. A content analysis of 700 humorous still images, memes, and cartoons demonstrates slight differences between the social media information environments. Humorous images in the Twitterverse tended to be slightly more partisan, invoke slightly more masculine stereotypes in portrayals of candidates, and were less likely to use emotionally evocative content. On both Twitter and elsewhere, humorous still images consisted largely of attacks and were relatively devoid of policy information. The results are explained in light of the nature of Twitter as a social media platform, specifically its character delimitation for text and the news orientation of its user base.

Keywords Twitter • Political humor • Partisanship • Gender stereotypes

T.L. Belt (✉)
Political Science, University of Hawai'i at Hilo, Hilo, HI, USA

John W. Kluge Fellow in Digital Studies, Library of Congress, Washington, DC, USA

© The Author(s) 2018   97
C.J. Galdieri et al. (eds.), *The Role of Twitter in the 2016 US Election*,
https://doi.org/10.1007/978-3-319-68981-4_7

INTRODUCTION

One of the unique features of the 2016 presidential election was Donald Trump's ability to politically "weaponize" his Twitter account in a way no other candidate had been able to do—using it to set the media agenda and to attack opponents with great effectiveness. While Facebook remains the largest social networking site, with 1.86 billion active users in the fourth quarter of 2016 (Statista 2017a) compared to Twitter's 319 million active users (Statista 2017b), research shows that Twitter is a different social media experience than other platforms. For example, a far greater number of Twitter users proclaim their interest in politics than Facebook users do (Gottfried 2014). Moreover, due to differing feed algorithms, those without an interest in politics are far less likely to see political content on Twitter than the politically uninterested on Facebook (Gottfried 2014). Additionally, scholars have noted a particular symbiotic relationship between news organizations and political campaigns on Twitter (Conway et al. 2015; Kwak et al. 2010; Parmelee 2013). The result is a highly politicized segment of the Twittersphere that provides a different social media experience than that found on other sites. What specific differences are there in the political information environment provided by Twitter as opposed to other social media platforms?

This study evaluates one subset of that universe of political discourse: political humor. Specifically, I examine the information environment created by the growing phenomenon of the use of still images as a means of political expression through social media. Through a content analysis of a sample of 700 images culled from social media platforms during the 2016 presidential campaign, this study compares the quality of discourse available to voters and tests several hypotheses regarding expected content on Twitter versus other media platforms. These expected differences include tone, partisanship, issue information, emotional content, the underscoring of candidates' personality traits, and the use of gender stereotypes.

THE EVOLVING RELATIONSHIP BETWEEN VOTERS AND ELECTRONIC MEDIA

Most voters never get a chance to meet presidential candidates, so until recently, their perceptions of those candidates had been based predominantly upon media portrayals. While interpersonal communication was important in shaping these perceptions (see Beck et al. 2002; Popkin

1991), it was believed that the ideas shared among the public predominantly came from a two-step flow—originating from mass media and then filtered through opinion leaders on to a wider public (Katz and Lazarsfeld 1955; Lazarsfeld et al. 1944). Today, these interpersonal dinner-table and water-cooler conversations have largely been replaced by social media, which has ended the overwhelmingly one-way flow of information.

This is not to say that social media has completely replaced broadcast media. During the 2016 election cycle, television remained the primary source for voters' news (57 percent). But a large segment of the population (38 percent) cited online sources (websites, social media, and apps) as their primary source for campaign news (Mitchell et al. 2016). Expectedly, the numbers were greater for younger people, with half of individuals between the ages of 18 and 49 citing online sources as their primary gateway for news. For those who got their news online, two-fifths reported social media as their primary source of information (Mitchell et al. 2016).

Clearly, the information environment in which candidates compete has drastically shifted in the recent years. Individual citizens have become gatekeepers in the larger information ecology by deciding what to post, repost, and link to on their social network accounts. The new influence of the common citizen in what we learn about politics stands in stark contrast to the bygone years of a top-down flow from broadcast networks through opinion leaders to individual voters. In addition to individual voters and news organizations, other actors including candidates, parties, and interest groups, attempt to influence the information environment through their social media presence. The result is a world of audio, visuals, and text that is fed to social media users in as many ways as there are individual users—each receiving a different "feed" of political messages.

As the media environment has become increasingly digitized, citizens are better able to interact with the information available to them, creating content and significantly affecting the feeds of other users. Can content transmitted through the new social media environment bring clarity and a flourishing of political discourse that educates citizens and enhances democracy? Or, is the digital environment doomed to bring out individuals' worst tendencies, leading to further political polarization and a degradation of the depth and breadth of policy discourse available to inform the citizenry? Does the type of digital environment matter in determining how the public learns about politics? Can humor help to cut across the partisan divide?

IMAGES, HUMOR, AND POLITICS IN SOCIAL MEDIA

Despite attempts to dismiss its importance, what happens in social media and other new digital venues can have an important influence on citizens (see Towner and Dulio 2011). This is because political media content frames issues, crystallizes opinions, develops and reinforces conceptions individuals carry of the candidates. This is particularly the case regarding perceptions of candidates' personalities, character traits, and issue positions (see Belt et al. 2007; Conover and Feldman 1989; Hacker 2004; Woodward 2006).

With its ability to disseminate political messages with little cost, the internet has become the primary battlefield in the contest over political ideas. The public and interest groups have become more engaged in the political process than ever before (see Kerbel 2009). The internet is changing the way in which the public thinks about politics, making democracy less of a spectator sport (Gainous and Wagner 2011). Elections offer an opportunity for increased political engagement and policy discourse, and presidential elections generate the most public interest and comment (see Just et al. 1996; Morton and Williams 2001; Owen 2008/09).

As the internet footprint of activist groups and individuals grows larger, there has been a commensurate decline in the power of traditional political institutions (Bimber 1998; Mele 2013). Individuals make use of social media platforms to voice their political positions and grievances. These expressions may be of their own authorship, may take the form of forwarded material from other sources, or may be some combination of the two.

However, the existence of internet content does not necessarily produce an audience. As always, viewers need a reason to "tune in" to content. Often, content that catches the public's eye and creates a "buzz" is content that entertains (boyd 2017). Other content that easily recirculates is information that confirms individual's political predispositions, which led to the propagation of "fake news" stories during the 2016 campaign (see Maheshwari 2016; Taub 2017).

Critical to creating likable content that entertains internet audiences is the use of humor (Belt 2015). Laughing at the powerful and those who aspire to power is a tradition that dates back at least to ancient Greece (Cronin 2014). A popular form of political humor is satire, which is based on exaggerating stereotypes (Morris 2009). Satire works comedically because it is based on a widely held version of the truth, or as *Saturday Night Live* (*SNL*) Executive Producer Lorne Michaels calls it: "heightened reality." It is stretching the truth that creates the humor. Humor is not politically trivial; it can grab and hold viewers' attention and decrease citizens' trust in governmental institutions (Baumgartner 2007).

Another concern for internet content that engages audiences is the use of visuals, which are more entertaining and attention grabbing than text alone (Belt 2003). Individuals tend to recirculate still images such as cartoons, "memes," and videos much more frequently than text-only content. Considering these trends, how did still images contribute to the information environment in the 2016 campaign? What did they contain and what effects did they have on our long-term perceptions of presidential candidates? Does the social media platform on which they were posted matter?

How Twitter Is Different

Twitter's famously short 140-character limit for "tweets" sets it apart from other social media platforms. The brevity of the format facilitates interaction, eliminating long pieces that are often ignored on social media.[1] As with other platforms, Twitter permits the embedded posting of still images and video. To facilitate this, Twitter has pioneered the use of "tiny URLs" that make it easier for users to fit external hyperlinks into their tweets in order to connect to information on other websites. But Twitter is different in other ways than just format.

One can tell a great deal about a social media platform by the profile of its users. After all, it is the users who create and recirculate content on these platforms. Demographic studies have found Twitter users tend to be slightly more urban and professional and to have higher incomes and higher levels of education than users of Facebook (see Greenwood et al. 2016; Molla 2016). Additionally, Twitter users are more likely to follow news outlets, to report regularly seeing news items, and to consider Twitter to be an important source of news than users of other social media networks (Molla 2016). The predominance of news on Twitter is what sets it apart from other social media platforms, as over 85 percent of topics tweeted are related to headline or persistent news items (Kwak et al. 2010). One scholar has even termed the seemingly constant background of news on Twitter feeds to be its own "ambient news network" (Hermida 2014).

Research on the use of Twitter by members of Congress shows that members seem to use Facebook and Twitter for largely the same reasons—position taking, advertising, and credit claiming. However, members were slightly more likely to share information about events on Facebook than Twitter (Lawless 2012). Other research finds that politicians use Twitter primarily to broadcast rather than to engage (Lyons and Veenstra 2016). These findings support the notion that candidates use Facebook to engage supporters and Twitter to talk to the press. The result is that Twitter has a greater air of professionalism than other sites. It is not surprising then that a study found that Senate candidates in 2010 were particularly positive and self-promotional in how they tweeted, with few negative tweets about their opponents (Bode et al. 2011).

HYPOTHESES

Given the findings of prior research studies, certain expectations can be made about the information environment created by the circulation of still images across Twitter versus other social media sites. The hypotheses are concerned with the quality of information that helps voters learn about and decide among political candidates. Information can be differentiated as attack or promotional and may be more or less partisan in content. Other information dimensions include the inclusion of candidates' policy issue positions and personality traits that signal to voters how each candidate might govern. Sadly, gendered stereotypes remain important cues in shaping how citizens evaluate candidates and how they are portrayed in media, and are also important to evaluate (see Cassese and Holman 2017; Conroy 2015). Finally, emotional content of media messages associated with candidates can stimulate information seeking, the diffusion of social media content, and can influence vote choice (Albertson and Gadarian 2015; Brady et al. 2017; Crigler et al. 2006; Just et al. 2007; Marcus et al. 2000).

The following hypotheses are based on the nature of the audience and the larger "news-y" culture of Twitter—it's higher level of education and income, greater level of professionalism, and greater level of consumption of and commenting on traditional "hard news." The hypotheses are also based upon prior research regarding the use of the medium by politicians as well as Twitter's format limits. While Twitter may be short, other social media sites are expected to be more brutish in nature,[2] lacking the editorial filtering that users would employ when anticipating an audience to be more professional and more likely to include members of the news media. Accordingly, the following hypotheses are proposed:

H1: Images circulated on Twitter will be more likely to address issues than images circulated on other sites.

H2: Images circulated on Twitter will be less conflictual than images circulated on other sites.

H3: Images circulated on Twitter will be less likely to use physical humor than images circulated on other sites.

H4: Images circulated on Twitter will be more likely to address personality traits associated with politicians than images circulated on other sites.

H5: Images circulated on Twitter will be less likely to invoke gendered stereotypes than images circulated on other sites.

H6: Images circulated on Twitter will be less emotionally evocative than images circulated on other sites.

DATA AND METHODS

The data for this study includes still images collected during the 2016 presidential campaign. Images were culled from the social media sites Facebook, Twitter, Instagram, and Tumblr, as well as the social media discussion boards 4chan, Imgur, Reddit, and FARK. On Facebook, three separate accounts were included to create different feeds—one conservative, one liberal, and one moderate. To be included in the sample, images must have been political in nature—referring to ideas or policy proposals that were prevalent during the campaign, attacking or promoting specific presidential candidates, commenting on candidates' appearances, personal or professional backgrounds, personalities, character traits. The images collected included manipulated photographs, photos with text added (also known as "memes"), screenshots of tweets, and other circulated images. Commercial political cartoons and still images of commercial broadcasts (such as from *Last Week Tonight with John Oliver*) that were shared on these sites were also collected. A total sampling frame of 1120 images was collected, from which 700 humorous images were randomly selected for inclusion into the content analysis.[3]

Each image was coded for the candidate(s) portrayed, policy information, tone and partisanship of the image, manipulations of the appearance of the candidate(s), personality traits, gendered stereotypes attributed to the candidate(s), and emotionally evocative content associated with each candidate. Coding was done both at the image level (characteristics of each image) and the individual level (characteristics of each political figure portrayed in each image). If an image made reference to or otherwise portrayed a policy issue, the issue domain was noted. Up to five issues were noted and coded per image. Other characteristics of each image coded included the tone of the image (attacking, neutral, or promotional) and the partisanship of the image was measured as a seven-point scale (strongly favoring Democrats to strongly favoring Republicans).

Up to five political figures were coded in each image (beyond five, a general "Republicans" or "Democrats" code was used). Individual-specific coding included the manipulation of a political figure's physical character- istics, such as reducing the size of Donald Trump's hands or stretching Hillary Clinton's nose to make her look like the Disney character Pinocchio. A variable for physical humor was created measuring whether or not the depiction of the individual political figure contained any such physical alterations at all.

Personality traits attributed to each political figure in the images were also coded, and these included items drawn from the American National Election Studies (ANES): knowledgeable, inspirational, experienced, pro- vides strong leadership, caring, honest, and "shares my moral values." Usually, coding for these items was easy—such as when an image of Donald Trump showed him misspelling a word (an indicator of less knowledge). A few times, this type of coding required a judgment on the part of the coder. In coding, every attempt was made not to read too much into an image. In doing so, coders were instructed to eschew Justice Potter Stewart's "I know it when I see it" means of assessment for something more akin to the *Miller* test: whether the common person, applying contemporary standards, would find that the work, taken as a whole, attributes a certain characteristic to a political figure (*Miller v. California* 1973, 413 U.S. 15). A variable for traits was created measuring whether or not the depiction attributed any such traits at all to the political figure.

In addition to physical and personality traits implied by the images, individual-level coding was done for masculine or feminine stereotypes associated with the political figures portrayed. Drawing on previous litera- ture, lists of both masculine and feminine stereotypes were drawn up, including both positive and negative stereotypes (sources for development of stereotype indicators: Bem 1974; Burke and Tully 1977; Conroy 2015; Helmreich et al. 1981; Huddy and Terklidsen 1993; Lawless 2004; Spence and Helmreich 1978; Spence et al. 1974, 1979). Masculine stereotypes included strong, confident, arrogant, cool, decisive, competitive, hostile, tenacious, aggressive, and dominant. Feminine stereotypes included passive, submissive, apologetic, approachable, caring, cooperative, selfless, emo- tional, whiny, and devoted.[4] Variables for masculine and feminine personality stereotypes were created to measure whether or not the depiction attributed any such traits at all to the individual appearing in the image.

The last individual-level measure coded was emotionally evocative content. Again, drawing upon items in the ANES, these emotions included enthusiastic, hopeful, proud, angry, afraid, and worried. A portrayal of an individual was coded as such if the depiction aroused a certain emotion either due to something said or done by the political figure (again, adopting ANES language). As with the other measures, a variable for emotionally evocative content was created to measure whether any such emotions at all were elicited in connection with the political figure depicted.

Finally, a reverse image lookup program (TinEye.com) was used to ascertain where the image appeared on the internet.[5] Almost all images were circulated across a variety of social media sites, so it was imperative to create a measure that could ascertain whether the image was circulated on Twitter. Accordingly, we coded the number of times a Twitter account appeared as a source in the top ten results reported back from TinEye.com. Although the results for the coding of the source of these images ranged from zero to ten Twitter sources, a little over half of the images (52.8 percent) did not appear on a Twitter account. In order to account for this skewness, a variable was created indicating whether the image appeared on Twitter at all in the first ten results. Training of coders required two sessions, between which time intercoder reliability improved from Kappa = .841 to Kappa = .960.

Results

Table 7.1 reports which of the political figures during the 2016 election cycle were portrayed in the images analyzed. Of the 700 images analyzed, 153 did not portray any political figures. Of the remainder, Donald Trump was clearly the favorite. Trump appeared in 46.1 percent of the 700 images and made up a sizeable 43.6 percent of the 740 individuals portrayed (multiple political figures could have been portrayed in each image). Hillary Clinton was a distant second, accounting for 110 portrayals, with Bernie Sanders taking the bronze medal with 41 portrayals. Other figures of note included Barack Obama (39 images), Ted Cruz (27 images), Melania Trump (20 images), Sarah Palin (14 images), and George W. Bush in 13 images. Other figures accounted for less than a dozen portrayals each (see Table 7.1).

A brief sketch of the information environment can be developed from the overall content of these images. In measuring the characteristics of the

Table 7.1   Political figures portrayed in images

Political figure	n	n as a percent of individuals portrayed
None	153	
Donald Trump	323	43.6
Hillary Clinton	110	14.9
Bernie Sanders	41	5.5
Barack Obama	39	5.3
Ted Cruz	27	3.6
Republicans	21	2.8
Melania Trump	20	2.7
Sarah Palin	14	1.9
George W. Bush	13	1.8
Jeb Bush	11	1.5
Marco Rubio	10	1.4
Michelle Obama	9	1.2
Debbie Wasserman Schultz	8	1.1
Mike Pence	8	1.1
Ben Carson	7	0.9
Chris Christie	7	0.9
Bill Clinton	7	0.9
Donald Trump Jr.	7	0.9
Carly Fiorina	5	0.7
Paul Ryan	4	0.5
Rudy Giuliani	4	0.5
Ivanka Trump	4	0.5
Jill Stein	4	0.5
John Kasich	3	0.4
Donna Brazile	3	0.4
Newt Gingrich	3	0.4
Gary Johnson	3	0.4
Eric Trump	3	0.4
Mike Huckabee	2	0.3
Democrats	2	0.3
Monica Lewinsky	2	0.3
Tim Kaine	2	0.3
Tiffany Trump	2	0.3
George H. W. Bush	2	0.3
Rush Limbaugh	2	0.3
Others (1 each)	8	1.1
Total	740	100.0

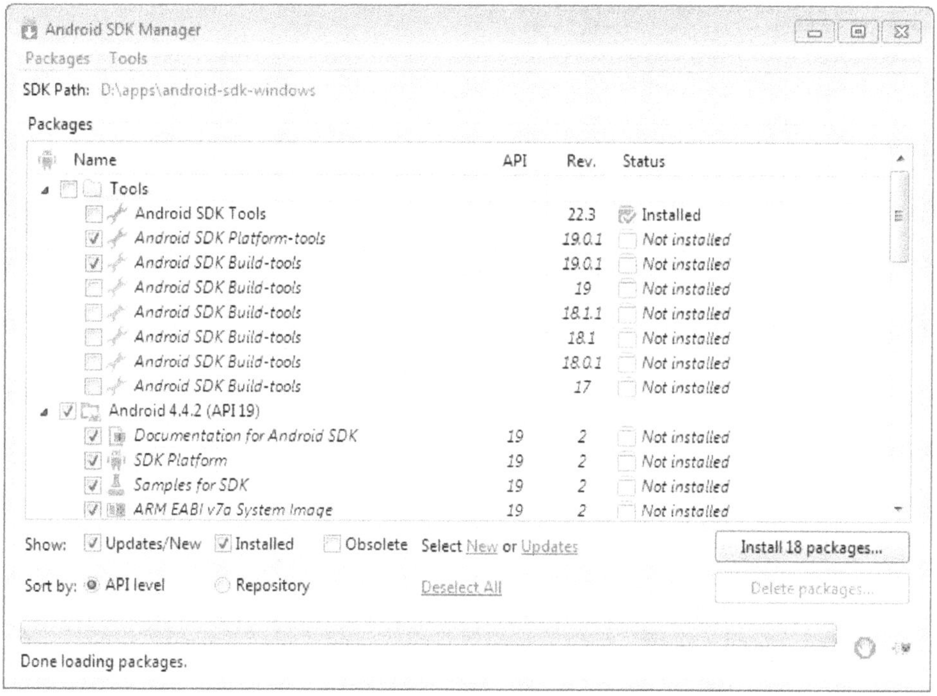

FIGURE 1-14. *SDK Manager with downloads selected*

have too much RAM for the standard development laptop. Figure 1-15 is a screenshot of the Create New Virtual Device dialog.

You can launch your new AVD from the Android Device Manager or from the command line. To launch from the command line, type `emulator -avd NameOfAVD`. The following is the command I use to launch my AVD named `NexusOne`:

```
emulator -avd NexusOne
```

Test your emulator by opening its web browser and navigating to a mobile page. http://maps.google.com/ and http://m.google.com/ are both examples of well-known mobile pages. While you are testing, make sure your Android emulator can access your local development workstation. From your emulator's web browser, try connecting to http://10.0.2.2/. From the emulator's perspective, this is your development workstation's IP address.

images, coding ranged from zero to one for the absence or presence of a certain characteristic. For the measure of issues, the mean value of 0.29 indicates that 29 percent of images dealt with a policy issue of any sort. Partisanship was recoded such that strongly or somewhat partisan images (scores 1–2 and 6–7) received a value of one and less-partisan or nonpartisan images (scores 3–5) received a value of zero. The result was that a majority of images, 80 percent, strongly or somewhat favored one party over the other. About three in ten of the images (29 percent) employed physical humor to depict a political figure, and a majority of the images (69 percent) ascribed certain personality traits to the figures. About a third of the images attributed masculine and feminine stereotypes to the subjects of the images (35 and 31 percent, respectively). Finally, 59 percent of images made use of emotionally evocative content tied to a political figure (see Table 7.2).

So, was Twitter different than other social media sites across these dimensions? Only slightly. The first hypothesis expected images circulated on Twitter to be more likely to address issues than images circulated elsewhere. This was not the case. In fact, images on Twitter were almost identical to images circulated elsewhere when it came to issues: 28.5 percent of images on Twitter and 28.9 per cent of images circulated elsewhere

Table 7.2 Characteristics of images

Variable	Mean	SD
Issues	0.29	0.45
Partisan	0.80	0.40
Physical humor	0.29	0.45
Personality traits	0.69	0.46
Male stereotypes	0.35	0.48
Female stereotypes	0.31	0.46
Emotional content	0.59	0.49

Table 7.3 Issues and source

	Not Twitter		Twitter	
	n	Percent	n	Percent
No issues	278	71.1	221	71.5
Some issues	113	28.9	88	28.5
Total	391	100.0	309	100.0

addressed issues ($\chi^2 = .015$, n.s.; see Table 7.3). The information environment provided by Twitter's users proved to be no more issue-rich than other social network venues.

The second hypothesis predicted that images circulated on Twitter would be less conflictual than images circulated on other sites. The coding data provided two measures for the relative conflictual nature of the images—tone (attacking versus support) and partisanship. The overwhelming majority of images, 89.1 percent, attacked a candidate. The prevalence of attacks was slightly, though not significantly, higher on Twitter than other social media sites (90.9 percent compared to 87.7 percent, $\chi^2 = 1.885$, n.s.; see Table 7.4). Contrary to expectations, images circulated on Twitter were slightly more likely to be partisan than images circulated on other sites. On Twitter, 83.2 percent of images were partisan, as compared to 78.3 percent of images circulated elsewhere, but this difference was not statistically significant ($\chi^2 = 2.644$, n.s.; see Table 7.5). This counterintuitive finding, small though it is, may have to do with the nature of Twitter—specifically, its tendency toward brevity, requiring messages to pack a more overtly partisan "punch" for effect.

The third hypothesis predicted that images circulating in the Twitterverse would be less likely to use physical humor in depictions of political figures than images circulating elsewhere. For this test, there was

Table 7.4 Tone and source

	Not Twitter		Twitter	
	n	Percent	n	Percent
Attack	343	87.7	281	90.9
Neutral	16	4.1	10	3.2
Support	32	8.2	18	5.8
Total	391	100.0	309	100.0

Table 7.5 Partisanship and source

	Not Twitter		Twitter	
	n	Percent	n	Percent
Nonpartisan	85	21.7	52	16.8
Partisan	306	78.3	257	83.2
Total	391	100.0	309	100.0

Table 7.6 Physical humor and source

	Not Twitter		Twitter	
	n	Percent	n	Percent
No physical humor	289	72.3	235	69.1
Some physical humor	111	27.8	105	30.9
Total	400	100.0	340	100.0

Table 7.7 Personality traits and source

	Not Twitter		Twitter	
	n	Percent	n	Percent
No personality traits	126	31.5	101	29.7
Some personality traits	274	68.5	239	70.3
Total	400	100.0	340	100.0

little difference between sources. Of the images circulated on Twitter, 30.9 percent included modifications to political figures' appearances in order to generate physical humor, as compared to 27.8 percent of images circulated elsewhere ($\chi^2 = 0.872$, n.s.; see Table 7.6).

In depicting the political figures, it was hypothesized that images circulated on Twitter would be more likely to address the personality traits of individuals than images circulated on other social media sites—that these images would do a better job of commenting on candidates' leadership capabilities. However, this was not the case. Images circulated on Twitter addressed the political figures' personality traits 70.3 percent of the time, as compared to 68.5 percent of the images circulated elsewhere ($\chi^2 = 0.278$, n.s.; see Table 7.7).

It was predicted that images on Twitter would make use of fewer gendered stereotypes in depicting political figures. This proved to be the case, as images depicting candidates on Twitter were less likely to invoke masculine stereotypes, with 30.6 percent of Twitter images doing so as compared to 39.3 percent of images circulated elsewhere ($\chi^2 = 6.040$, $p < .05$; see Table 7.8). In terms of feminine stereotypes, images on Twitter were similar to images circulated elsewhere, with 31.8 percent of Twitter images invoking feminine stereotypes of candidates compared to 31.3 percent of images elsewhere ($\chi^2 = 0.023$, n.s.; see Table 7.9). It is likely that, similar to broadcast media coverage, feminine stereotypes are still

Table 7.8   Masculine stereotypes and source

	Not Twitter		Twitter	
	n	Percent	n	Percent
No masculine stereotypes	243	60.8	236	69.4
Some masculine stereotypes	157	39.3	104	30.6
Total	400	100.0	340	100.0

Table 7.9   Feminine stereotypes and source

	Not Twitter		Twitter	
	n	Percent	n	Percent
No feminine stereotypes	275	68.8	232	68.2
Some feminine stereotypes	125	31.3	108	31.8
Total	400	100.0	340	100.0

Table 7.10   Emotions and source

	Not Twitter		Twitter	
	n	Percent	n	Percent
No emotional content	151	37.8	151	44.4
Some emotional content	249	62.3	189	55.6
Total	400	100.0	340	100.0

considered "fair game" for commentary on Twitter, whereas masculine stereotypes are less so.

Finally, it was expected that images circulated on Twitter would be less emotionally evocative than images circulated on other sites. This tended to be the case, as 55.6 percent of images on Twitter were emotionally evocative, as compared to 62.3 percent of images circulated on other sites. This 6.7 percent difference suggested a slight degree of support for the hypothesis ($\chi^2 = 3.377$, $p = .066$; see Table 7.10).[6] So, although images on Twitter were slightly more partisan in their messaging, the appeals made in the images were less emotional in nature.

CONCLUSION

The 2016 election was featured heavily in social media. Supporters of candidates of all stripes were able to make their voices heard through social media (including the Green and Libertarian parties). There are many political uses and gratifications that users glean from such interaction. Some may be trying to shepherd their friends to a position of supporting their preferred candidate. Others may be making performative statements about their identity, allegiances, and their outlook on the world (see Rentschler and Thrift 2015). Still others derive a sadistic enjoyment in "trolling" other users (Buckels et al. 2014; Sest and March 2017).

The nature of a social network's user base interacts with its functionality in order to produce a distinct social networking experience. Different news feeds, text limitations, and content posting features cause Twitter and Facebook to contribute to the political information environment in different ways. The content and functionality of each makes political expression easier on Facebook, while surveillance of the political news landscape is easier on Twitter. So how might this have impacted what people learned during the 2016 election?

To a large degree, the information that users could glean from still images manufactured and recirculated by other users (comics, memes, etc.) was largely the same on Twitter as on other social network sites. Policy information was sparse everywhere, and the vast majority of images were used to attack political figures (particularly the presidential candidates). But the Twitterverse showed some slight differences as compared to other social networks. Images were just as likely to be attacks, but were slightly more partisan and yet less emotionally evocative. Moreover, depictions of candidates circulated on Twitter engaged in less masculine stereotyping than images on other social network sites. So, to some degree, the images on Twitter were slightly more likely to make cooler, more rational appeals in attacking candidates, likely for consumption by members of the news media.

The differential use of gender stereotypes raises an interesting question: Why were there fewer masculine stereotypes used on Twitter as opposed to other social media sites, but a similar number of feminine stereotypes? Part of the answer has to do with the nature of the 2016 campaign. Donald Trump was not a prototypical politician. His displays of arrogance and braggadocio were highly unusual. Unique, too, were his tendencies to interrupt his opponents during debate (particularly Hillary Clinton), and to shout them down with yells of "WRONG!" into his microphone (again, especially Hillary Clinton). In a sense, 2016 was a "hyper-masculine" election year, and these masculine stereotypes were on the minds of voters. Content creators are limited by the materials with which they have to work, and Trump provided a lot of stereotypical masculine material. The use of these crude masculine stereotypes peaked on other social media sites, but was slightly moderated on the "mainstream-newsier" Twitter.

A reason why the use of feminine stereotypes was equal across social media sites is likely due to the fact that these stereotypes are still (unfortunately) considered legitimate points of political discussion, even in a more news-oriented social media platform. Additional research and more data are required to tease out if gender stereotyping disproportionately affected one candidate over another. Prior research would indicate that these images may have disproportionately affected the female candidates in the election (see Belt 2012; Cassese and Holman 2017).

To a large degree, the still images found on Twitter are similar to the images found on other social networks. This may be due to the fact that many social network users do not limit themselves to one network. The result is an increase in the likelihood that particularly appealing images will be shared across more than one social media platform, reducing the variance across platforms. This may be likely to continue as technology continues to make doing so easier.

The election of 2016 may indeed have been the "Twitter" election. It helped lesser-known candidates catch fire. It helped to vault one (Sanders) from relative obscurity to almost winning his newly adopted party's nomination, and it helped to take another (Trump) all the way to the presidency. While networks like Facebook and Twitter have vast user bases and may be around for a very long time, it is equally possible that another social media platform will become "the next big thing" and cause us to re-think the political implications of social media. At this time, however, the media platforms available to the general public are used for attacks. Most of the circulated imagery—and a picture is worth a thousand words—is used to tear down opposition rather than to promote a favored candidate. Instead of laughing *with* one another at politicians, we are laughing *at* one another across the partisan divide. The humor analyzed here shows a pattern of punching down and degradation of others in the form of political attacks.

While negativity can play an important role in providing issue content and stimulating information seeking (see Lau et al. 2007), the data analyzed here were relatively issue-poor. However, the still images did provide a significant amount of information regarding the personality traits of candidates, which are important for predicting candidates' future behavior (see Barber 2008). It remains to be seen if social media can be used as a megaphone and debating stage for common citizens, or if its users will continue to create and recycle content that mimics information available elsewhere in the media universe. It is likely that Donald Trump's politically successful Twitter style of attacks will be mimicked by candidates and voters for years to come. If that is the case, usage of social media will continue to be predominantly to attack opponents (Trump's *modus operandi*), and the use of humor can be counted on to intensify the sting rather than lessen the blow. We are not yet ready to laugh together.

Acknowledgments The author is indebted to Madison Ferris, Ananya Hariharan, Tyler Hoffman, and Sarah Momsen-Jones for research assistance.

NOTES

1. It is true that some people have found ways to post longer treatises on Twitter, by indicating that they will use multiple tweets as a thread, or to write a longer passage and to take a screen shot of it and attach it as an image file. Still, Twitter largely does not suffer the TL;DR (too long; didn't read) problem of other social media platforms.
2. Apologies to Thomas Hobbes.
3. Humorous images outnumbered non-humorous images by a ratio of 5:1. The non-humorous images were found to be largely similar to the humorous images across all variables and were removed from the analysis in order to focus exclusively on humorous images, maintaining consistency for the proposed hypotheses.
4. Yes, some of these are horribly sexist and offensive.
5. TinEye.com was found to be more reliable than other reverse-lookup programs such as Google, which resulted in a great deal of false-positive identifications.
6. For a sample size of $n = 740$, the $p < .10$ threshold attained here could be considered significant.

REFERENCES

Albertson, Bethany, and Shana Kushner Gadarian. 2015. *Anxious Politics: Democratic Citizenship in a Threatening World*. New York: Cambridge University Press.

Barber, James David. 2008. *Presidential Character, the: Predicting Performance in the White House*. 4th ed. New York: Routledge.

Baumgartner, Jody C. 2007. Humor on the Next Frontier: Youth, Online Political Humor, and the 'Jib-Jab' Effect. *Social Science Computer Review* 25 (3): 319–338.

Beck, Paul Allen, Russell J. Dalton, Steven Greene, and Robert Huckfeldt. 2002. The Social Calculus of Voting: Interpersonal, Media, and Organizational Influences on Presidential Choices. *American Political Science Review* 96 (1): 57–73.

Belt, Todd L. 2003. *Metaphor and Political Persuasion*. PhD Dissertation, University of Southern California, Los Angeles.

———. 2012. Viral Videos: Reinforcing Stereotypes of Female Candidates for President. In *Women and the White House: Gender, Popular Culture, and Presidential Politics*, ed. Justin Vaughn and Lilly Goren, 205–226. Lexington: The University Press of Kentucky.

———. 2015. Is Laughter the Best Medicine for Politics? Commercial Versus Noncommercial YouTube Videos. In *Controlling the Message: New Media in American Presidential Campaigns*, ed. Victoria A. Farrar-Myers and Justin S. Vaughn, 200–218. New York: New York University Press.

Belt, Todd L., Ann N. Crigler, and Marion R. Just. 2007. *Affective Priming in the 1996 Presidential Campaign*. Paper presented at the Annual Meeting of the American Political Science Association, Chicago, August 30–September 2.

Bem, Sandra L. 1974. The Measurement of Psychological Androgyny. *Journal of Consulting and Clinical Psychology* 42 (2): 155–162.

Bimber, Bruce. 1998. The Internet and Political Transformation: Populism, Community, and Accelerated Pluralism. *Polity* 31 (1): 133–160.

Bode, Leticia, David Lassen, Young Mie Kim, Travis N. Ridout, Erika Franklin Fowler, Michael Franz, and Dhavan Shah. 2011. *Putting New Media in Old Strategies: Candidate Use of Twitter During the 2010 Midterm Elections*. Paper presented at the Annual Meeting of the American Political Science Association, Seattle, September 1–4.

boyd, danah. Hacking the Attention Economy. *Points.* Last updated January 5, 2017. https://points.datasociety.net/hacking-the-attention-economy-9fa1daca7a37#.nr36brwv6

Brady, William J., Julian A. Willis, John T. Jost, Joshua A. Tucker, and Jay V. Van Bavel. 2017. Emotion Shapes the Diffusion of Moralized Content in Social Networks. *Proceedings of the National Academy of Sciences*, 1–6. http://www.pnas.org/content/early/2017/06/20/1618923114.full

Buckels, Erin E., Paul D. Trapnell, and Delroy L. Paulhus. 2014. Trolls Just Want to Have Fun. *Personality and Individual Differences* 67: 97–102.

Burke, Peter J., and Judith C. Tully. 1977. The Measurement of Role Identity. *Social Forces* 55 (4): 881–897.

Cassese, Erin C., and Mirya R. Holman. 2017. Party and Gender Stereotypes in Campaign Attacks. *Political Behavior* 39: 1–23. https://link.springer.com/article/10.1007/s11109-017-9423-7

Conover, Pamela Johnston, and Stanley Feldman. 1989. Candidate Perception in an Ambiguous World: Campaigns, Cues, and Inference Processes. *American Journal of Political Science* 33 (4): 912–940.

Conroy, Meredith. 2015. *Masculinity, Media, and the American Presidency.* New York: Palgrave Macmillan.

Conway, Bethany A., Kate Kenski, and Di Wang. 2015. The Rise of Twitter in the Political Campaign: Searching for Intermedia Agenda-Setting Effects in the Presidential Primary. *Journal of Computer-Mediated Communication* 20 (4): 363–380.

Crigler, Ann N., Marion R. Just, and Todd L. Belt. 2006. The Three Faces of Negative Campaigning: The Democratic Implications of Attack Ads, Cynical News and Fear Arousing Messages. In *Feeling Politics: Affect and Emotion in Political Information Processing*, ed. David P. Redlawsk, 135–163. New York: Palgrave Macmillan.

Cronin, Thomas E. 2014. Laughing at Leaders (American Politicians Especially). *Leadership and the Humanities* 2 (1): 27–43.

Gainous, Jason, and Kevin Wagner. 2011. *Rebooting American Politics: The Internet Revolution.* New York: Rowman & Littlefield.

Gottfried, Jeffrey. Facebook and Twitter as Political Forums: Two Different Dynamics. *Pew Research Center.* Last modified November 12, 2014. http://www.pewresearch.org/fact-tank/2014/11/12/facebook-and-twitter-as-political-forums-two-different-dynamics/

Greenwood, Shannon, Andrew Perrin, and Maeve Duggan. Social Media Update 2016. *Pew Research Center.* Last updated November 11, 2016. http://www.pewinternet.org/2016/11/11/social-media-update-2016/

Hacker, Kenneth L., ed. 2004. *Presidential Candidate Images.* New York: Rowman & Littlefield.

Helmreich, Robert L., Janet T. Spence, and John A. Wilhelm. 1981. A Psychometric Analysis of the Personal Attributes Questionnaire. *Sex Roles* 7 (11): 1097–1108.

Hermida, Alfred. 2014. Twitter as Ambient News Network. In *Twitter and Society*, ed. Katrin Weller, Axel Bruns, Jean Burgess, Merja Mahrt, and Cornelius Puschmann, 359–372. New York: Peter Lang.

Huddy, Leonie, and Nayda Terkildsen. 1993. Gender Stereotypes and the Perception of Male and Female Candidates. *American Journal of Political Science* 37 (1): 119–148.

Just, Marion R., Ann N. Crigler, Dean E. Alger, Timothy E. Cook, Montague Kern, and Darrell M. West. 1996. *Crosstalk: Citizens, Candidates, and the Media in a Presidential Campaign.* Chicago: University of Chicago Press.

Just, Marion R., Ann N. Crigler, and Todd L. Belt. 2007. Don't Give Up Hope: Emotions, Candidate Appraisals and Votes. In *The Affect Effect: Dynamics of Emotion in Political Thinking and Behavior*, ed. W. Russell Neuman, George E. Marcus, Ann N. Crigler, and Michael B. MacKuen, 231–259. Chicago: University of Chicago Press.

Katz, Elihu, and Paul Felix Lazarsfeld. 1955. *Personal Influence: The Part Played by People in the Flow of Mass Communications*. New York: Free Press.

Kerbel, Matthew R. 2009. *Netroots: Online Progressives and the Transformation of American Politics*. Boulder: Paradigm.

Kwak, Haewoon, Changhyun Lee, Hosung Park, and Sue Moon. 2010. What Is Twitter, a Social Network or a News Media? *Proceedings of the 19th International Conference on World Wide Web*, 591–600.

Lau, Richard R., Lee Sigelman, and Ivy Rovner. 2007. The Effects of Negative Political Campaigns: A Meta-analytic Reassessment. *Journal of Politics* 69 (4): 1176–1209.

Lawless, Jennifer L. 2004. Women, War, and Winning Elections: Gender Stereotyping in the Post-September 11th Era. *Political Research Quarterly* 57 (3): 479–490.

———. 2012. Twitter and Facebook: New Ways for Members of Congress to Send the Same Old Messages? In *iPolitics: Citizens, Elections, and Governing in the New Media Era*, ed. Richard L. Fox and Jennifer M. Ramos, 206–232. New York: Cambridge University Press.

Lazarsfeld, Paul Felix, Bernard Berelson, and Hazel Gaudet. 1944. *The People's Choice: How the Voter Makes Up His Mind in a Presidential Campaign*. New York: Columbia University Press.

Lyons, Benjamin A., and Aaron S. Veenstra. 2016. How (Not) to Talk on Twitter: Effects of Politicians' Tweets on Perceptions of the Twitter Environment. *Cyberpsychology, Behavior, and Social Networking* 19 (1): 8–15.

Maheshwari, Sapna. 2016. How Fake News Goes Viral: A Case Study. *New York Times*. November 20. https://www.nytimes.com/2016/11/20/business/media/how-fake-news-spreads.html

Marcus, George E., Michael MacKuen, and W. Russell Neuman. 2000. *Affective Intelligence and Political Judgment*. Chicago: University of Chicago Press.

Mele, Nicco. 2013. *The End of Big: How the Digital Revolution Makes David the New Goliath*. New York: Picador.

Mitchell, Amy, Jeffrey Gottfried, Michael Barthel, and Elisa Shearer. The Modern News Consumer: News Attitudes and Practices in the Digital Era. *Pew Research Center*. Last modified July 7, 2016. http://www.journalism.org/2016/07/07/the-modern-news-consumer/

Molla, Rani. Social Studies: Twitter vs. Facebook. *Bloomberg Gadfly*. Last modified February 12, 2016. https://www.bloomberg.com/gadfly/articles/2016-02-12/social-studies-comparing-twitter-with-facebook-in-charts

Morris, Jonathan S. 2009. The Daily Show with Jon Stewart and Audience Attitude Change During the 2004 Party Conventions. *Political Behavior* 31 (1): 79–102.

Morton, Rebecca B., and Kenneth C. Williams. 2001. *Learning by Voting*. Ann Arbor: University of Michigan Press.

Owen, Diana. 2008/09. Election Media and Youth Political Engagement. *Journal of Social Science Education* 7/8(2/1): 14–24.

Parmelee, John H. 2013. Political Journalists and Twitter: Influences on Norms and Practices. *Journal of Media Practice* 14 (4): 291–305.

Popkin, Samuel L. 1991. *The Reasoning Voter: Communication and Persuasion in Presidential Campaigns*. Chicago: University of Chicago Press.

Rentschler, Carrie A., and Samantha C. Thrift. 2015. Doing Feminism in the Network: Networked Laughter and the 'Binders Full of Women' Meme. *Feminist Theory* 16 (3): 329–359.

Sest, Natalie, and Evita March. 2017. Constructing the Cyber-Troll: Psychopathy, Sadism, and Empathy. *Personality and Individual Differences* 119: 69–72.

Spence, Janet T., and Robert L. Helmreich. 1978. *Masculinity and Femininity: Their Psychological Dimensions, Correlates, and Antecedents*. Austin: University of Texas Press.

Spence, Janet T., Robert L. Helmreich, and Joy Stapp. 1974. The Personal Attributes Questionnaire: A Measure of Sex-Role Stereotypes and Masculinity-Femininity. *JSAS Catalog of Selected Documents in Psychology* 4: 43–44.

Spence, Janet T., Robert L. Helmreich, and Carole K. Holohan. 1979. Negative and Positive Components of Psychological Masculinity and Femininity and Their Relationships to Self-Reports of Neurotic and Acting Out Behaviors. *Journal of Personality and Social Psychology* 37 (10): 1673–1682.

Statista. 2017a. Twitter: Number of Monthly Active Users 2010–2017. https:// www.statista.com/statistics/282087/number-of-monthly-active-twitter-users/. Accessed 27 June 2017.

———. 2017b. Facebook: Number of Monthly Active Users Worldwide 2008–2017. https://www.statista.com/statistics/264810/number-of-monthly-active-facebook-users-worldwide/. Accessed 27 June 2017.

Taub, Amanda. 2017. The Real Story About Fake News Is Partisanship. *New York Times*. January 11. https://www.nytimes.com/2017/01/11/upshot/the-real-story-about-fake-news-is-partisanship.html?smid=tw-upshotnyt&smtyp=cur

Towner, Terri L., and David A. Dulio. 2011. The Web 2.0 Election: Does the Online Medium Matter? *Journal of Political Marketing* 10 (1–2): 165–188.

Woodward, Gary C. 2006. *Center Stage: Media and the Performance of American Politics*. New York: Rowman & Littlefield.

INDEX

Note: Page number followed by 'n' refers to notes.

© The Author(s) 2018   119
C.J. Galdieri et al. (eds.), *The Role of Twitter in the 2016 US Election*,
https://doi.org/10.1007/978-3-319-68981-4